The Dictionary of 1980s Slang

STRANGER THAN FICTION!
THE TOTALLY AWESOME GUIDE TO ROCKIN' '80S LINGO

FROM THE AUTHOR OF THE USA **#1** BEST-SELLING (UNOFFICIAL) SCRABBLE BOOK "THE DICTIONARY OF TWO-LETTER WORDS"

RICK CARLILE

CARLILE
MEDIA

The Dictionary of 1980s Slang
Stranger than Fiction! The Totally Awesome Guide to Rockin' '80s Lingo

By Rick Carlile

Cover art and illustrations by Rick Carlile

First edition published 2021 by Carlile Media, Las Vegas, NV
Published in the United States of America

ISBN-13: 978-1-949117-21-9
ISBN-10: 1-949117-21-9

Library of Congress Control Number: 2021941436

www.CARLILE.MEDIA

A DIVISION OF CREADYNE DEVELOPMENTS LLC

Table of Contents

List of Figures

Introduction

Why do we love slang so much? Throughout history people have treasured the vivid, imaginative, ingeniously hilarious, often viciously caustic words and phrases that make up our private languages.

Slang is the language of liberty. Free of tedious rules, it is a natural way to evade the clutches of authority figures who try to control us. We invent it, seek it out, and employ it intuitively. Slang is innovation, improvisation, discovery, performance, street stand-up. As a secret code of insiders, used by people in every walk of life from surfers and students to drug dealers and doctors, slang cannot simply be learned – it must be earned.

Poets receive the benefit of "poetic license," but slang is totally unlicensed language, speeding on a stolen metaphor, a contemptuous linguistic scofflaw. Slang is eloquent vulgarity.

Every decade of the twentieth century had a distinct, unique character. Influenced by world events, technological advances, social changes and evolving tastes, this cultural spirit manifested itself most tangibly in our popular media. There is no better way to understand the personality of a culture or era than by studying its media, and the core of media is language.

Standard language alone does not tell us much, as by definition it changes little in the space of a few years or decades. On the other hand, slang exists to define that which is new, different, improved. Slang tells us what people believe is important in their lives. It embellishes and embroiders the things about which we care deeply. By examining this nonstandard language we can grasp the soul of the time, the zeitgeist.

The character of the 1980s was overwhelmingly positive, audacious, brash, fearless. Despite or perhaps because of the constant looming threat of nuclear annihilation posed by the US-USSR Cold War, the spirit of the decade unapologetically pushed the sliders to maximum across the board. Bigger. Brighter. Louder. Faster. Harder. More, more, MORE!

Some people may denounce this as meaningless hedonistic excess. Perhaps, to an extent. But mainly this attitude is mistaken. Hedonism is thoughtless pleasure, and there was nothing thoughtless about the power behind '80s exuberance. That power came from justified self-belief, the joy of life and potency that tells you to do it because you can and because life is short but sweet. Who needs irony? It's nothing but a shield for the uncertain and fearful. Be *serious* in your art, your fashion, your music, your business, your life. Serious fun. Go for it. Get it. And when you've got it, flaunt it.

'80s slang tells us all this. It lauds the positive and exceptional with absurd hyperbole, derides the negative and tawdry with utter savagery. It is full of new concepts and new ways of thinking from fresh, revolutionary disciplines as varied as home computing and hip hop.

This dictionary strives not only to be a piece of enjoyable nostalgia but also to provide some insight into what made the 1980s great. It might even remind us of a few things we used to know but have since overlooked.

It has been difficult to decide what to include and what to exclude, and some veterans of the decade may search in vain for terms that were used in their part of the world, their subculture or clique. They may find undue weight given to surf or hip hop slang, Californian dialect, and so forth. But this book is an examination of the mass culture, the mainstream, and those are the phenomena that influenced that dominant culture. There is a good reason that California, home and haven of the positive thinker, monopolized the media and minds of the era.

It's worth taking a moment to remember how different life was during the 1980s. We were on the cusp of the Information Age, but while many people eagerly employed the new home computers for entertainment and education only a few were using them for communication. Radio, newspapers, television, and – above all – movies were how we received our information. Our friends were local folks who we'd see in the street every day, except perhaps for one or two across the country or pen pals in another part of the world with whom we'd communicate by handwritten letter.

This all sounds abominably restrictive to the modern ear, but it didn't feel that way. There seemed nothing strange or inadequate about waiting all week so you could sit down at a specific time to see a certain TV show. Media was everywhere, as it is today, with the difference that it came to us not person to person or on demand but piped through monolithic, monocultural broadcast organizations.

That's not to say there was no alternative. Underground scenes of the 1980s were truly exciting! One couldn't simply discover all about a subterranean or controversial band, nightclub, book, or movie at the click of a button. The lure of the unknown, exotic and dangerous, communicated by word of mouth and bootleg tapes, created a visceral thrill of exploration and discovery.

Like technologies, attitudes change over time. Many ways of speaking and thinking from past decades can seem today to be inconsiderate or cruel. Also, much slang is deliberately acerbic; it is not a genteel art form. It is therefore necessary to resist the temptation to gloss over this for the sake of politeness, to bowdlerize the lexicon or downplay the everyday prevalence of things that we may now find distasteful – or things that were intentionally distasteful at the time! It would be a disservice to the reader to do so, robbing the language of its impact, and these words and phrases are included without apology (though, I hope, with a degree of sensitivity).

The entries in this book adhere to the following format, including pronunciation guides where useful and providing citations from popular culture. These citations are given not only to demonstrate the correct employment of the slang and to prove its authentic use during the decade, but also to serve readers with a tidbit from a cultural artifact of the period that may send them off on a pleasant journey of (re-)discovery. Within definitions, bold small capitals indicate cross-references to terms also defined in the dictionary. Italics identify parts of speech and citations (to avoid confusion, italics are not used for other purposes).

headword[1]   *part of speech*[2] Description, **REFERENCED TERM**. *"Citation." (From "source," date.)*

Provided citations are sourced from media with release dates up to and including 1990 and, rarely, '91 or '92,[3] as movies, albums, etc. often take years to grind their way through the production process. Citations for song lyrics and other short, readily available sources are provided by reference (for example, "*Ref. 'Jungle Love' by Morris Day and The Time, 1984*"). Long-source and hard-to-find, obscure citations are provided in full.

It has also been a matter of some debate where to draw the line on the inclusion or exclusion of older slang terms, many of which were used for many decades prior to the '80s. **DUDE** is a prime example; one could hardly omit it from a dictionary of '80s slang, yet it has been in documented common use since the 1880s. Generally, therefore, a term is included if it remained in significant mainstream American use during the target decade.

Finally, readers who are too young to remember the avaricious '80s may find it tricky to **GET YOUR ARMS AROUND** the **MIND FRAME** of goal-oriented materialism best exemplified by the **YUPPIE**, that proud icon of this most conspicuously consumerist decade. To that end, this book includes an educational card game that you can cut out (or photocopy, if you do not wish to damage the book) and play, suitable for all ages. Focused on the cutthroat acquisition of all manner of fashionable and stylish consumer products, you will find it at the end of the book under the title "The Yupper Hand."

Be **EXCELLENT** to each other!

---

1. Initial apostrophes ('burbs, 'nads, 'rents, 'roids, etc.) are omitted from headwords for the sake of readability. Other initial punctuation, such as "-" for suffixes, is retained.
2. Parts of speech are given in simple format; i.e., "verb" rather than "phrasal verb." Gerunds are listed as nouns.
3. With one example from 1994, demonstrating how an '80s slang expression had already fallen from use.

ABC gum *noun* Pre-owned chewing gum: "Already Been Chewed." A mysterious schoolyard initialism often used to trick unsuspecting younger kids. *"I felt and probably looked like a piece of ABC gum." (From "Mystery at Bluff Point Dunes" by Lisa Eisenberg, 1988).*

absotively *adverb* A highly affirmative response: portmanteau of "absolutely" and "positively." *"You're positive?" "Absotively!" (From "Mannequin," 1987.)*

ace *adjective* Excellent, slick, neat, exceptional, topflight, best-in-class. *"You're still the ace degenerate." (From "The Karate Kid," 1984.)*

acid house *noun* A subgenre of **HOUSE** music, also known simply as "acid," developed by Chicago DJs in the mid-1980s and wildly popular at parties and raves in the late '80s. Acid house spread from Chicago to London, UK, before making it back across the Atlantic to find popularity in New York, Detroit, and then the rest of the world. Opinion is divided as to the origin of the term. Some attribute it to Chicago acid house group Phuture's 1987 "Acid Trax" 12-inch, considered by many to be the first acid house record. Others, notably British musician Genesis P-Orridge, contend that the term was coined by British musician Genesis P-Orridge. *"Suddenly, Acid House culture blossomed into a heady mix of sex, drugs, and dance." (From "Spin" magazine, January 1989.)*

acid-washed *adjective* Of denim, to have been subjected to an industrial process of tumbling with pumice stone and chemicals (initially bleach, later potassium permanganate) to achieve a unique, high-contrast, mottled appearance. These jeans and denim jackets emulated the bleach-spattered appearance of **PUNK** clothing and achieved mainstream ubiquity by the mid-1980s. See also **STONE-WASHED, DESIGNER JEANS.** *"He wears a calf-length denim coat, acid-washed jeans, and an artfully torn ALL-AMERICAN HERO T-shirt." (From "New York" magazine, April 1988.)*

adult child *noun* The "adult child" movement of the 1980s was one of the various therapeutic concepts popular at the time. It concentrated on its patients' "arrested development," caused by early trauma, and their consequent "failure to launch" (i.e., leave the nest; see **BOOMERANG KID**). As with many other similar movements it received widespread criticism for its perceived self-absorption and pathologizing of "normal" human experience: as psychologist and author of "The Diseasing of America" Dr. Stanton Peele put it, "They're all at these meetings, complaining about how they were treated as children. [...] Meanwhile, their kids are at home. You wonder what groups they're going to go to when they grow up." (Baltimore Sun, October 10, 1992).

aerobicize *verb* To engage in the trendy activity of aerobics: instructor-led exercising and stretching intended to improve cardiovascular health, flexibility, joint strength, and overall well-being. Aerobics became extremely fashionable in the 1980s, following the release of the "Jane Fonda's Workout" video in 1982, and provided an opportunity to wear neon-colored leotards, spandex leggings, and giant puffy leg warmers. Women's clothing was even more outrageous. Despite being considered a low risk activity aerobics can be dangerous. In 1984 iconic artist Patrick Nagel, whose sharp, graceful, dramatic "Nagel women" portraits captured the look and attitude of the 1980s more elegantly than any other's work, sadly passed away at the age of thirty-eight after a fifteen-minute charity fundraising "aerobathon," due to an undiagnosed heart defect. *"I want her to live, I want her to breathe. I want her to aerobicize." (From "Weird Science," 1985.)*

Fig. 1: Portrait of a Woman (After Patrick Nagel)

after-hours *adjective* Descriptive of an entertainment establishment often of dubious legality that continues to sell alcohol after closing time at more reputable bars and clubs. Also ("After Hours") Martin Scorsese's sinister, darkly humorous 1985 tour of New York's **WEIRDO** night-dwellers.

-age *suffix* Suffix appended to a word indicating either the totality of objects or concepts exhibiting the pertinent quality or belonging to the relevant class, or a specific instance thereof. Such words function in the same manner as the standard-usage "roughage": "that (food-stuff) which is rough." California origin. See **GRINDAGE**, **TUNEAGE**, also **DOOBIE** ("doobage").

ain't no thang *phrase* No big deal, no problem. Used both in a polite, dismissive sense ("Hey, no problem,") and also to indicate that something is easy for the speaker, either without affectation or as a brag. *(Ref. "Hit Me" by Nice & Smooth, 1989.)*

air guitar *noun* Imaginary instrument, the playing of which requires extremely vigorous rock 'n roll or **HEAVY METAL** stage performance moves such as headbanging, power-stancing, windmilling, knee slides, the Chuck Berry duck walk, and the like. Air guitar playing began as a dancefloor/gig phenomenon among rock fans and **HEAD-BANGER**s, as celebrated/parodied in the "Bill & Ted" movies' Wyld Stallyns air guitar licks. It later became an entertainment form in its own right. As with many such phenomena, an educational handbook on the subject could be purchased (see citation). *"Remember that the air guitar has size and shape." (From "The Complete Air Guitar Handbook," by John McKenna and Michael Moffitt, 1983.)*

airhead *noun* One whose head is full of air. A gender-neutral slur, being appropriately applied to both the football **JOCK** and the **VALLEY GIRL** cheerleader. *"[I] thought she was your usual airhead bitch." (From "Heathers," 1989.)*

all the way live *adjective* Of an event or occurrence: energetic, wild, and fun ("live" as in "live wire," "live music"). *"So like Andrea's sweet sixteen party was like all the way live." (from "Fer Shur! How to Be a Valley Girl – Totally!" by Mary Corey and Victoria Westermark, 1982.)*

amped *adjective* **STOKED**, **PSYCHED**, **HYPE**d up. Electrified, energized about something or other. Derived from the electrical unit of current "ampere" and/or "amplifier," both of which are commonly shortened to "amp." Possibly connected to amphetamines ("speed"). *(Ref. "Fight the Power" by Public Enemy, 1989.)*

AMW *noun* "Actress, Model, Whatever." A struggling wannabe performer or bona fide Z-list female celebrity or, euphemistically and cruelly, a prostitute. Refers to the many Hollywood hopefuls waiting for their big breaks or fallen on hard times but still keeping up appearances. *"Either in Los Angeles or New York there is a young actress, model, whatever, called Toy." (From "Designs: a Novel" by James Brady, 1986.)*

angel dust *noun* Popular street name for the illegal (since 1978) hallucinogenic drug phencyclidine (phenylcyclohexyl piperidine, PCP). PCP was the subject of significant media concern in the late 1970s, persisting into the early 1980s, but soon supplanted in infamy by the crack cocaine epidemic beginning in the early to mid-1980s (see **CRACK, ON** and **BASE**). As in the citation, by the later '80s the now-dated term could be used to humorously imply an obsolete, **NOWHERE** attitude; the moral panic around the character's other concern, switchblade knives, is best exemplified by the venerable 1957 musical "West Side Story." *"I've seen a lot of bullshit – angel dust, switchblades." (From "Heathers," 1989.)*

apeshit *adjective* Frenzied with wild excitement. Acting with delirious, demented abandon. Also extremely angry, crazed with fear, or out of control due to the influence of any other emotion. See also **BATSHIT**. *"We who are about to go apeshit salute you!" (From "Bachelor Party," 1984.)*

Aqua Velva geek *noun* A **DISCO** lecher. The sort of guy who calls himself a "swinger" and wears satin shirts open to the navel to show off his gold tone medallion. Still to be found in the 1980s, shambling around forlornly trying to **SCORE** with girls many years his junior like a zombie who doesn't know he's dead already. The term derives from the once-popular aftershave of the same name, with which such types would attempt to overpower their victims. **VALSPEAK**. See also **GEEK**. *"So, like this totally grody Aqua Velva geek is in the mall, and, like, he is sooo beige." (From "Stein's Way: Editorial Cartoons" by Ed Stein, 1983.)*

artfag *noun* Insulting term[1] for anyone perceived by the accuser to be less **HARDCORE** than himself in a musical or stylistic context. One who listens to **NEW WAVE** or **NEW ROMANTIC** bands, particularly British ones. Pretentious **ATTITUDE**, **BOHO** clothing, **MCJOB** (in the citation-referenced lyrics the speaker mocks his interlocutor for claiming to go to chic, arty parties while actually working at fast food restaurant Hardees). Definitely not a bona fide professional artist, merely a hanger-on or pretender. *(Ref. "Instant Club Hit (You'll Dance to Anything)" by The Dead Milkmen, 1987.)*

as if *interjection* A negative response in **VALSPEAK** indicating disbelief ("As if that could be true!") or disgust ("As if I would do that!")

attitude *noun* In a positive sense, a forceful personality; energetic confidence. Often used as "(word) with attitude" to indicate a particularly, large, impressive, aggressive or fundamentally **COOL**er example of something (synonymous with "(word) on ste**ROIDS**"). For the negative sense, see **BAD ATTITUDE**.

automagical *adjective* Marketing and technical term for a laborsaving system that takes minimal user input and, via a clever, seemingly miraculous process, produces a desired result. Portmanteau of "automatic" and "magical." *"'File Scanner' processes and displays prepared text files automagically." (Advertisement for "Instant Replay" software from "PC" magazine, June 24, 1986.)*

awesome *adjective* Widely-used expression denoting approval in any degree from near-indifference to eternal love. May or may not

---

1. See **FAG** for the distinction in meaning between the traditional and 1980s teen usages of the root word.

indicate the actual inspiration of awe. *"We are some awesome monster bashers!" (From "The Lost Boys," 1987.)*

axe *noun* Musician's slang for a guitar, particularly in hard rock and **HEAVY METAL**, due to the somewhat similar shape of the instrument and the important fact that axes are **COOL**. Also applied to other instruments, less commonly and in other musical genres' subcultures; specifically the saxophone/sax, due to the phonetic similarity. Also "ax." *"We'll take these axes." (From "The Blues Brothers," 1980.)*

babe *noun* An attractive female. Usually intended as a compliment, though not always received as such. Also an affectionate nickname for one's romantic partner (male or female). *"Finland babes!" (From "Earth Girls are Easy," 1988.)*

baby Benz *noun* The Mercedes-**BENZ** W201 (190/190D/190E) sedan, manufactured from 1982 and available in the North American market from 1983. The German company's first compact automobile and, though not cheap, a comparatively affordable entry point to the brand. As implied by the citation, a serious competitor to BMW's popular 3 Series (see **BEEMER**). *"The new 'baby Benz' has been long awaited. Now the company is finally starting to fight BMW." (From "The Black Enterprise Auto Guide for 1984," "Black Enterprise" magazine, November 1983.)*

back in the day *phrase* In a past time, particularly in reference to a period regarded as a classic era or golden age. Generally used with a sense of nostalgia or at least that things were better then, in one way or another. See also **OLD-SCHOOL**. *(Ref. "Wild Wild West" by Kool Moe Dee, 1987.)*

bad *adjective* Good. An example of linguistic "amelioration," where a negative word develops a positive meaning (see also **WICKED**, **SICK**). Some consider the term a contraction of the synonymous **BADASS** (adj.), but this is unlikely as "bad" has been recorded in this positive sense since 1897; the connection is more likely the other way around. When applied to a person the term implies a dangerous, ruthless quality. When describing an object the implication is of **AWESOME** design/artistry, raw power, and similar admirable characteristics. Also the title track of Michael Jackson's 1987 album. The video for "Bad" was initially intended to feature Prince; however, the artist declined the offer due to issues with the lyrics, reportedly telling Jackson, "The first line of that song is 'Your butt is mine.' [...] Who's gonna sing that to whom? 'Cuz you sure ain't singing it to me, and I sure ain't singing it to you." Superlative: "baddest." *(Ref. "Bad" by Michael Jackson, 1987.)*

badass *noun* A person not to be messed with on account of his or her competitive abilities and combative **ATTITUDE** either in the brute physical sense or in some other field of endeavor. As an adjective describing a person or thing who is, without doubt, **BAD**. *"There seem to be this discrepancy between badass music and really being a badass." (From "I Need More: The Stooges and Other Stories" by Iggy Pop, 1982.)*

bad attitude *noun* Catchall phrase used by figures of authority to describe a range of perceived personality defects in a subject, including arrogance, infantility, passive aggression, aggressive passivity, smugness, churlishness, willfulness, evasiveness, hubris, apathy, etc. In effect, this boils down to the subject either (a) unfairly and mistakenly believing the authority figure to be an idiot, or (b) justly and accurately knowing the authority figure to be an idiot. Also simply "attitude"[1] or "tude." *"Mahoney, park this car! [...] Do it now or you're fired, you understand? Fired!" "That's not fair. The guy has a bad attitude." (From "Police Academy," 1984.)*

bad to the bone *adjective* Descriptive of one who is not just **BAD** but a complete and utter uncompromising **BADASS**. Bad through and through. *(Ref. "Bad to the Bone" by George Thorogood and the Destroyers, 1982.)*

bagbiter *noun* Poorly designed or executed computer software or hardware, which fails to function in a manner a reasonable user would expect. Also the person or people responsible for producing the product in question. Also "bite the bag": to crash or fail. The 1983 Jargon File (see **FLAME**) describes the term's origin thus: "The original meaning of this term was almost undoubtedly obscene, probably referring to the scrotum. In its current usage it has become almost completely sanitized."

bag on *verb* To cast aspersions on or insult someone or something, usually in a kidding way and/or at some length, entertainingly riffing on the theme. Derivation unclear, but probably related to "bag" in the hunting or competitive sense (to place vanquished prey in one's game bag): to conquer and thus own the target. *(Ref. "Play it Kool" by Kool G Rap & DJ Polo, 1990.)*

bag your face *verb* **VALSPEAK** expression indicating that the speaker finds the targeted person less than appealing. May refer to facial appearance, in which case the suggestion is that placing a paper sack over the head may hide the excrescence from view. More often the criticism is directed at another aspect of one's presentation (such as dress) or behavior (such as commission of some particularly embarrassing act), in which case the suggestion is that face-bagging might hide one's shame. Also simply "Bag it."

bail *verb* To leave rapidly; originates from the act of "bailing out" of an aircraft in an emergency, but used more succinctly: "We gotta bail."

ball and chain *noun* Marriage in general, one's spouse in particular. A reference to the physical restraint device or shackle affixed to prisoners between the 17th and mid-20th centuries and beloved of unimaginative editorial cartoonists. *"It was when you started introducing me as 'the old ball and chain.' That's when I left." (From "Ghostbusters II," 1989.)*

ball-huggers *noun* Tight swimming trunks on a male. *"You see, all those beach blanket boppers in their bikinis and ball-huggers are being menaced by monsters." (From "Danse Macabre" by Stephen King, 1983.)*

---

1. For the positive sense, see **ATTITUDE**.

ballistic *adjective* Describes a peak level of incandescent rage at which the channeled propulsive power of one's fury is sufficient to sustain an intercontinental parabolic trajectory, achieving exo-atmospheric altitude at apogee, unleashing multiple reentry vehicles to rain thermonuclear fire onto the target. Extremely angry. Popularized by use of the phrase "go ballistic" in "Top Gun" (1986), though its usage in that movie was incorrect. Far from referring to achieving maximum performance, the phrase is used of an aircraft or other flying object that is no longer under guidance (i.e., it is either out of control due to misadventure, or its propulsion source has cut out by design). An aircraft that has "gone ballistic" is therefore merely an unguided projectile, at the mercy of gravity and other environmental forces. See also the footnote under **HEAVY METAL**. *"We're going ballistic, man. Go get him!" (From "Top Gun," 1986.)*

bang *verb* To have sex with. Also to engage in gang-related activity. See also **GANG BANG**. In computing (noun) a synonym for "exclamation point." *"Did she get to you, huh? Did you bang her?" (From "The War of the Roses," 1989.)*

banging *adjective* Extremely good, particularly in relation to an event, experience, or member of the opposite sex ("bangin' **BOD**").

barf *verb* To vomit. Onomatopoeic. Also the name of the half-man, half-dog "mawg" ("I'm my own best friend!") in the 1987 Mel Brooks sci-fi spoof "Spaceballs," played by the great John Candy. In computing, to crash or fail. See also **-O-RAMA**. "**SCARF** and barf" refers to the actions of one suffering from an eating disorder; see **GAG ME WITH A SPOON**. *"As you know, I am the Barf Inspector. [...] Barf Inspector comin' through." (From "Porky's II: The Next Day," 1983.)*

barf bag *noun* A disposable airsickness containment bag, provided by airlines to passengers, into which they may vomit if the need arises. Often branded with the airline's name and logo, which seems like counterproductive marketing. By extension, a disgusting or repugnant person, particularly a criminal lowlife type. *"You're a big barf bag." (From "Poltergeist," 1982.)*

barf me out *interjection* **VALSPEAK** exclamation indicating that the previous piece of sensory input was so disgusting, unpleasant to consider, or otherwise objectionable that further contemplation would likely **GROSS ME OUT** to the point of emesis. Like **GAG ME WITH A SPOON**, but more emphatic. Also "Barf me **OUT THE DOOR**," referring to the strong reactive force of such a powerful expulsion. *"Like, all those sweaty bods. Barf me out." (From "Valley Girl," 1983.)*

barf-o-rama *noun* See **-O-RAMA**.

Barney *noun* A clueless **DOOFUS** or uninteresting "stock" type character. Also cop jargon for a small-town police officer or "local yokel" (after Barney Fife from "The Andy Griffith Show"). *"What's a Barney?" "It's like [...] haole[1] to the max." (From "North Shore," 1987.)*

---

1. A non-Hawaiian person; often used insultingly, implying **DORK**-ishness.

base *noun* Freebase or pure cocaine, processed using ether to remove the hydrochloride present in powdered cocaine. Though similarly smoked in a pipe, freebase differs chemically from crack cocaine. Crack, which is safer to produce (using ammonia rather than ether, which is highly inflammable and forms explosive vapor) replaced freebase cocaine in the market. The terms "freebase" and its derivatives (such as "freebasing," using the drug) thus came to refer also to crack. *(Ref. "The Boomin' System" by LL Cool J, 1990.)*

base (first, second, third) *noun* Euphemistic description of goal achievement in the dating game, via baseball. First base: French kissing. Second base: exploratory manipulation. Third base: oral sex. Home run: full intercourse, and the crowd goes wild. *"So ... am I gonna get to first base?" (From "Fast Times at Ridgemont High," 1982.)*

batcaver *noun* An old-school **GOTH**. Likely originates from "The Batcave," the first goth club in London, UK, opening in Dean Street, Soho, in 1982.

batshit *adjective* To be or go completely crazy, exhibiting totally irrational behavior. Also "bat shit." While "batshit" shares aspects of meaning with **APESHIT**, the two are not synonymous: one can be batshit insane in a very quiet, self-possessed way, whereas going apeshit demands extroversion. *"First time I heard 'bat shit,' I really came apart. [...] Aw! Bat shit. (laughter)." (From "Filthy Words" by George Carlin, transcribed in "Media Concentration: Hearing Before the Subcommittee on General Oversight and Minority Enterprise of the Committee on Small Business," House of Representatives, January 21, 1980.)*

B-boy *noun* A practitioner of breakdancing (see **BREAKDANCE**). Also "B-girl" and "breaker." The "B" stands for "break." *"B-boys [are] what you call break boys.... Or b-girls, what you call break girls." (Afrika Bambaataa)*

BBS *noun* "Bulletin Board System." The first incarnation of the public Internet, accessible via archaic technologies such as Telnet (a text-only "terminal" program). BBSes were the precursor not only of email and other messaging, but of discussion forums and, much later, social media. BBSes generally died out with the advent of inexpensive dial-up Internet access and the Web browser in the early 1990s.

beastie *noun* A **SCUZZ**y or **GRODY** person or situation. Sometimes, of a person, used in a fairly affectionate sense. Also "beasty." *(Ref. "Valley Girl" by Frank Zappa, 1982.)*

beatbox *verb* To engage in a form of vocal percussion where sound effects (generally, though not always, mimicking drum sounds) are generated by the human larynx, mouth, tongue, etc. rather than using the more traditional Roland TR-808 drum machine (from which the term "beat box" derives). As a noun, a practitioner of beatboxing. The title of "first human beatbox" is contended by several artists including Darren Robinson, Doug E. Fresh, and others. The technique rose in popularity alongside the early '80s **HIP HOP** phenomenon as up-and-coming artists could not afford the expensive high-tech rhythm machines and made do with what was available to them. The inclusion of beatboxer and "Man of 10,000 Sound Effects" Michael Winslow in the 1984 movie "Police Academy" and its many, many wonderful sequels (as cadet Larvell Jones) did much to popularize the art form. *(Ref. "My Buddy" by DJ Jazzy Jeff & the Fresh Prince, 1988.)*

beatdown *noun* A savage and embarrassing thrashing, typically administered by multiple assailants to a single victim, for ostensibly corrective purposes. *(Ref. "Critical Beatdown" by Ultramagnetic MCs, 1988.)*

Beemer *noun* A BMW automobile. The BMW was the quintessential early 1980s **YUPPIE**mobile, so the proud owner naturally required an easy-to-say abbreviation to use while loudly yakking about it at downtown stoplights on his brick-sized **CELLULAR**. *"You get a make on that red Beemer yet?" (From "Lethal Weapon 2, 1989.)*

beeper *noun* An electronic paging gadget, also known as a "pager" or "radio pager," precursor to the cell phone. Popular among drug dealers, who would need to receive orders from customers when already out and about. Therefore, an accessory seen as an indicator of criminal status (in either a positive or negative sense, depending on the beholder). The device would monitor a radio broadcast stream from a central system transmitter and, on receiving a message containing its unique identifying code, display the phone number of the caller who wished to talk to the pager's owner. The owner could then find a pay phone and converse with the original caller. *(Ref. "6 'N the Morning" By Ice-T, 1987.)*

beer goggles *noun* Metaphorical eyewear, referring to the capacity of alcohol to modify the human visual perception, specifically its amplification of the attractiveness of potential dates and mates. *"'Time to strap on the beer goggles,' Engelstad announces." (from "Life on the Rim: a Year in the Continental Basketball Association" by David Levine, 1989.)*

beige *adjective* Boring, old-fashioned, tedious, dull, insipid. Back in the 1970s it was considered sophisticated for almost everything to be colored beige, except for one's bathroom.[1] Consequently the 1980s pastel-neon rebel alliance against these earth tones was as vitriolic and violent as the contemporaneous and famously ruthless anti-**DISCO** backlash. *"So, like this totally grody Aqua Velva geek[2] is in the mall, and, like, he is sooo beige." (From "Stein's Way: Editorial Cartoons" by Ed Stein, 1983.)*

bells and whistles *noun* Features of a computer program or other manufactured product which are of only tangential utility but which are included either to attract the customer directly, to enable marketing claims that accomplish the same purpose, or to feed the ego of those involved in the product's development. According to the 1983 Jargon File (see **FLAME**) "Nobody seems to know what distinguishes a bell from a whistle." The citation demonstrates not only the questioner's amusing ignorance of the phrase but also the disdain in

---

1. A stylish 1970s bathroom would be avocado, burnt orange, harvest gold, or some mix thereof.
2. See **AQUA VELVA GEEK**.

which such features are rightly held for causing unnecessary complexity, loss of operational focus, and cost/time overruns. *"General MALONEY: '[The claim that] the system has many bells and whistles – that is false. [...] It doesn't have bells and whistles. [...] We didn't add a thing to this program once we published the requirement document in 1978.' Mr. STRATTON: 'What is [sic] the bells and whistles supposed to refer to?' General MALONEY: 'I don't know, sir.' Mr. STRATTON: 'The computer whistles every time it gets a target?' General MALONEY: 'The comment as I remember in the article was that the Army had added bells and whistles and made it a very complex system. Not so.'" (From "Defense Department Authorization and Oversight Hearings on HR 2287 (HR 2269)" by United States Congress House Committee on Armed Services, March–April 1983.)*

Benz, Benzo *noun* A Mercedes Benz automobile. Arguably a superior machine to the BMW (see **BEEMER**) but, while popular, not quite so greatly favored by the **YUPPIE** crowd (except for the SL and similar high-end models, for those with serious money). *(Ref. "Something About My Benzo" by Sir Mix-A-Lot, 1989.)*

Betamax *noun* Early 1980s home video cassette format backed by Sony. Loser of the home video format wars to **VHS** due to its greater expense and comparative user-unfriendliness. Anyone whose family had purchased Betamax equipment would be roundly derided by his or her peers and ostracized, their plaintive arguments about Beta's technical superiority ignored. As an adjective, the term could even be used to disparagingly imply poor quality or general loserishness (synonymously with **BOOTLEG**). *"If you can afford a television, now you can afford a Betamax." (Sony advertisement in "Texas Monthly" magazine, April 1984)*

Betty *noun* An attractive female. Originally older surf slang deriving either from 1960s "The Flintstones" character Betty Rubble or 1950s pinup model Bettie Page (though, since the term carries a "good girl" connotation, the Rubble connection is more likely). *(Ref. "Out Goin' Cattin'" by Sawyer Brown, 1986.)*

BFF *noun* One's "Best Friend Forever." Not contractually enforceable.

BFI *noun* "Brute Force and Ignorance." Particularly in computing and engineering, a problem solving approach requiring little thought, imagination, skill, or knowledge. Frustratingly to those who value such qualities, the BFI approach tends to solve problems at least as effectively as more nuanced techniques and often more quickly – though usually less efficiently, with zero elegance. *"The less conscientious tend to approach the problem with Brute Force and Ignorance (BFI), and use the convenience of the program to avoid the more painful exercise of thinking." (From "Proceedings, Volume 5" by the American Society for Engineering Education, 1988.)*

biggie *noun* See **NO BIGGIE**.

big hair *noun* Any of a variety of voluminous 1980s hairdos relying on perming, curling, back-combing, vast quantities of environmentally hostile hairspray, etc. Initially prominent in the '80s among women with an interest in country & western music and its associated culture, big hair was massively popularized by the Texas-based

TV soap "Dallas." For males, big hair was favored by those involved with or emulating the "hair metal" musical genre (an evolution of **GLAM**). Big hair also became the standard for 1980s professional women as part of the fashion for **POWER DRESSING**, not only for the impressive "lion's mane" effect but out of a necessity to visually balance the ever-expanding shoulder pads of feminine office wear, lest one appear tiny-headed. *(Ref. "Western Girls" by Marty Stuart, 1989.)*

bigtime *adverb* Extremely, to a great extent, to a professional or otherwise impressive level. Also a strong affirmative. *"Carlino is heavy. I mean, bigtime." (From "Armed and Dangerous," 1986.)*

big whoop *interjection* Sarcastic expression indicating that the speaker is unimpressed by the intended gravity of what he or she has just heard. *"'C'mon, you guys. I'm including you in my act.' 'Big whoop,' said Joey, and he sat down on my bed." (From "The Amazing Valvano and the Mystery of the Hooded Rat" by Mary Robinson, 1989.)*

bikini wax *noun* Hair removal around the female inguinal area to enable the wearing of a bikini without the unsightly appearance of "spider legs" sticking out. Another form of rebellion against the hirsute 1970s (see **DISCO**). **VALSPEAK.** *"Full-leg (including bikini) wax, was $38, now $20." (From "Sales & Bargains" by Leonore Fleischer, "New York" magazine, September 14, 1981)*

billys *noun* Folding money, or money in general. From "bills." **VAL-SPEAK.**

bimbette *noun* Like a **BIMBO** but physically or mentally more diminutive. An attractive and flirtatious but apparently **AIRHEAD**ed young or petite female. Disparaging. *"I know this eighteen-year-old bimbette that's just gorgeous." (From "Wall Street," 1987.)*

bimbo *noun* Originally Italian for a (young) male child and used by authors such as P. G. Wodehouse to describe vapid young men, the term's diminutive focus switched in the latter half of the twentieth century to refer to females perceived as not only **AIRHEAD**ed but also exaggeratedly blonde and pneumatic (or at least scantily or provocatively dressed).

bitchin' *adjective* Very cool, deserving of great respect. Derives from "son-of-a-bitchin.'" Also "bitchen." *(Ref. "Bitchin' Camaro" by The Dead Milkmen, 1985.)*

bite *verb* To **RIP OFF**, steal, or imitate something – particularly another, more successful artist's act. A habit of the weak-minded and unscrupulous. *(Ref. "Sucka MCs" by Run-DMC, 1984.)*

bite me *interjection* A derisive exclamation indicating contempt for the target's opinion, feelings, or point of view. Derives from "Bite my ass!"

biter *noun* A contemptible person, particularly an artist, whose act is derivative rather than original; a thief or imitator of other's works See **BITE**. *(Ref. "Braggin' & Boastin'" by Jungle Brothers, 1988.)*

bizarro *adjective* Bizarre, but more so. Spectacularly weird. Also employable as a noun – a strange person or thing: "Who was that bizarro I saw you with?" *"This wouldn't be that bizarro thing you were babbling about over the phone last night?" (From "Heathers," 1989.)*

blar *noun* **"blaaar"** An overweight person. Pronounced in a long, drawn-out fashion, expressing the total ennui characteristic of the junk food gourmandizer or couch vegetator at his or her lowest energy level (see **VEG OUT, COUCH POTATO**).

blaze up *verb* To ignite marijuana (or, rarely, another drug) in one form or another. *"Yo, wastoid, you're not gonna blaze up in here!" (From "The Breakfast Club," 1985.)*

blitz *adjective* To get high on drugs and/or alcohol. Usually expressed as "get blitz" – not "get blitzed" as one might expect, though that form was also in vogue at the time, particularly in **VALSPEAK**. Also a London, England nightclub that ran only from 1979–80 but whose "Blitz Kids" were credited with (or blamed for) the birth of the **NEW ROMANTIC** movement. *(Ref. "Dead Homiez" by Ice Cube, 1990.)*

blood *noun* Appellation expressive of a strong friendship resulting in kinship. A brother from another mother. Also a friendly expression for any person (particularly male, particularly Black, particularly young.) *"Oh, Stewardess? I speak Jive. [...] Just hang loose, blood." (From "Airplane," 1980.)*

blow chunks *verb* To vomit, **BARF**, **RALPH**. Derives from the consistency of the emitted matter combined with the velocity of its ejection. *"Do not attempt to go out to the bar and get smashed until you blow chunks (there will be plenty of time to do that on game day)." (From "The Michigan Journal," University of Michigan-Dearborn, 1984.)*

blow off *verb* To skip; to deliberately not show up to an event, usually something onerous or boring like a class. *"Let's blow off this kissy-face garbage and get right to the good stuff!" (From "The Modern Guide to Sexual Etiquette for Proper Gentlemen and Ladies" by Turnbull & Willoughby, 1987.)*

BMX *noun* The oxymoronically-named sport of "bicycle motocross" ("Bicycle Moto-X") developed in the 1970s on a parallel track with motocross racing, particularly in California. As kids began to emulate their engine-equipped elders, using robust single-speed bicycles, they developed a riding style featuring spectacular stunts, jumps, thrills and spills. In the early to mid-1980s the sport made the jump into the commercial mainstream, boosted by movies such as 1986's "Rad" and the Australian "BMX Bandits"[1] (1983). *"You know what we've gotta get?" "Yeah, lost." "Not if we got our own BMX track." (From "BMX Bandits," AKA "Short Wave," 1983.)*

---

1. Released as "Short Wave" in the US, a reference to the walkie-talkies featured in the movie. Presumably this was due to the debatable assessment that "BMX" was not a widely recognized initialism across the wider US at the time.

Fig. 2: BMX Key Features

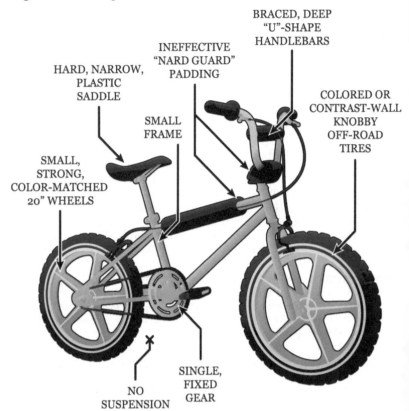

BRACED, DEEP "U"-SHAPE HANDLEBARS

INEFFECTIVE "NARD GUARD" PADDING

HARD, NARROW, PLASTIC SADDLE

COLORED OR CONTRAST-WALL KNOBBY OFF-ROAD TIRES

SMALL FRAME

SMALL, STRONG, COLOR-MATCHED 20" WHEELS

SINGLE, FIXED GEAR

NO SUSPENSION

bod *noun* Abbreviation of "body." Usually used in a positive, approving way. *"Hi, Ferris, how's your bod?" (From "Ferris Bueller's Day Off," 1986.)*

bodacious *adjective* Extremely impressive due to supreme size, excellence, beauty, or other superlative qualities. Likely a portmanteau of "bold" and "audacious." Finding widespread popularity due to its use in the 1982 movie "An Officer and a Gentleman" and soon thereafter used to excellent effect in the "Bill and Ted" movies, many assumed this to be a 1980s-coined neologism. Nonetheless, the term dates back to at least the 1840s Deep South, when one Georgia writer complained, "She's so bowdacious unreasonable when she's riled." This spelling gives weight to the earlier origin hypothesis, being a slight corruption of a possible original "boldacious." *"Ted, you and I have witnessed many things, but nothing as bodacious as what just happened." (From "Bill & Ted's Excellent Adventure," 1989.)*

boffo *adjective* Outstanding, successful, particularly of a movie or other piece of commercial pop culture. Onomatopoeic in origin, per "hit movie," "box office smash," etc. An example of "Variety-speak,"[1] a form of showbiz insider slanguage emanating from and popularized over many decades by Hollywood trade publication "Variety." The magazine joyfully employed initially opaque but highly efficient headlines, such as 1935's "Sticks Nix Hick Pix" (rural audiences react negatively to movies about rural life). *"I got this boffo, socko script for a Broadway slot called 'Manhattan Melodies.'" (From "The Muppets Take Manhattan," 1984.)*

Bogart *verb* To hog or monopolize something, particularly a marijuana joint. Refers to actor Humphrey Bogart's on-screen habit of leaving a cigarette burning in the corner of his mouth, apparently forgotten, rather than paying it due attention. *"Lovechild shoved herself against me and pouted, 'Don't Bogart! Don't Bogart! It's expensive!'" (From "Killer on the Road" by James Ellroy, 1986.)*

bogue *adjective* Contraction of **BOGUS**, with identical meaning. Also (verb) to smoke a cigarette (after Humphrey **BOGART**).

bogus *adjective* Not good; bad (in its traditional sense; not **BAD**). Only a slight change in meaning from its standard use: something fake or fraudulent. Originally from the (African) Hausa language "boka" meaning "to fake." In computing, anything that is nonfunctional, useless, false, unbelievable, or silly is "bogus." Derivative words include "bogosity" (the degree to which something is bogus), "bogon" (a unit or particle of bogosity, or a person or thing exhibiting bogosity), "bogometer" (instrument for measuring or displaying bogosity levels), and "quantum bogodynamics" (a field of study dedicated to explanation of the functioning of the universe in terms of bogon emitters, sinks, fields, etc.) *"What Jefferson was saying was, 'Hey! We left this England place cuz it was bogus.'" (From "Fast Times at Ridgemont High," 1982.)*

boho *adjective* Bohemian, in outlook or dress (hippie or gypsy). Also (noun) an artistic type. Note: an **ARTFAG** might dress boho, but a true boho is not generally an artfag.

bohunk *noun* Derogatory term for a person of Central or Eastern European extraction. Derives from "BOhemian" (Czech) and "HUNgarian." Not related to **HUNK**. *"Lay off, he's just a kid, ya big dumb bohunk." (From "Adventures in Babysitting," 1987.)*

boink *verb* To have sex with (someone). *"I'm supposed to sit here and discuss my mental health with a man who refers to the act of human procreation as 'boinking'?" (From the "Moonlighting" episode "The Straight Poop," 1987.)*

Bolivian marching powder *noun* Powdered cocaine (as distinct from free**BASE** or crack cocaine). Derives from the drug's typical geographical origin (more generally, in South America) and its capacity to imbue the user with apparently superhuman reserves of energy and enthusiasm (to be repaid with interest the following day). *"Your brain at this moment is composed of brigades of tiny Bolivian soldiers. They are tired and muddy. [...] They need the Bolivian Marching Powder." (From "Bright Lights, Big City" by Jay McInerney, 1984.)*

---

1. Subject of the 1993 "Animaniacs" song of the same name.

bomb *noun* Usually "the bomb." Something very good, excellent. Also (verb) to graffiti a wide array of surfaces as rapidly as possible with little regard for artistic quality.

bomb-diggity *noun* Completely unnecessary elaboration of **BOMB** carrying no additional meaning whatsoever.

bone *verb* To take the active role in sexual intercourse. Derives from the priapic "boner." *"I think the girls are looking for a long, lean bone job from me." (From "Weird Science," 1985.)*

bonus *interjection* Exclamation: great, terrific, excellent.

boof *verb* To engage in backdoor intercourse, particularly in a homosexual manner. From **BU-FU**.

booger *noun* Derogatory term for an unusually unattractive person. Also a general-purpose insult. From the original meaning, "snot." *"Dad says you're gonna be late again, you booger!" (From "Fast Times at Ridgemont High," 1982.)*

boogie *verb* To get moving, beat feet. *"Let's boogie." (From "The Blues Brothers," 1980.)*

book *verb* To get out of somewhere rapidly and abruptly. Etymology is unclear; the usage may relate to booking out of a hotel, booking passage on a ship, moving so fast you make the record books, or – most likely – signing a logbook to leave a military base; "book out" (something one would be likely to do with great alacrity when issued a weekend pass). *"They're coming out of the goddamn walls! Let's book!" (From "Aliens," 1986.)*

boombox *noun* An infernal device consisting of stereo speakers, radio, and one or more **TAPE** cassette decks. Carried on the shoulder of a group's most muscular member much in the manner of an infantry radio operator. The boombox, played at deafening volume, was a fixture of any summertime outdoor gathering throughout the 1980s. Particularly popular among both the **PUNK** and **HIP HOP** communities.

Fig. 3: Boombox Anatomy

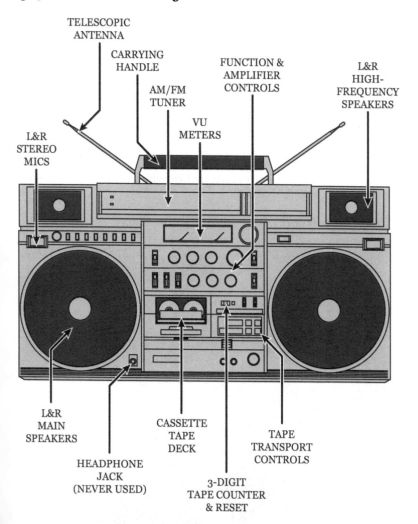

TELESCOPIC
ANTENNA

CARRYING
HANDLE

AM/FM
TUNER

FUNCTION &
AMPLIFIER
CONTROLS

L&R
HIGH-
FREQUENCY
SPEAKERS

VU
METERS

L&R
STEREO
MICS

L&R
MAIN
SPEAKERS

HEADPHONE
JACK
(NEVER USED)

CASSETTE
TAPE
DECK

3-DIGIT
TAPE COUNTER
& RESET

TAPE
TRANSPORT
CONTROLS

boomerang kid *noun* Adult offspring who fails to adequately spring off. One who, having left the family nest, returns some time later, usually for financial reasons. *"The phenomenon of the boomerang kid is too recent for anyone to have had much experience with what happens to them." (From "Adweek's Marketing Week" magazine, 1988.)*

bootleg *adjective* Off-brand, **GENERIC**, not the genuine article. Similar to **BOGUS** but less harsh. The term originated in prohibition-era smugglers' habit of concealing bottles of illegally-obtained liquor in the shafts of their boots. The defined usage derives from the term's more recent mainstream application: an unsanctioned recording of a band or musical artist made from within the audience at a live concert, using smuggled-in Radio Shack equipment. These cassette TAPEs may look exciting when purchased from a music pirate but when taken home and examined more closely will turn out to be completely unlistenable. *(Ref. "Carnival World" by Jimmy Buffett, 1989.)*

boss *adjective* Of superlative quality. Resurgent 1960s slang.

bounce *verb* To leave. An action achievable without personal effort by means of a bouncer (see **BUM-RUSH**).

bow-head *noun* "boe-head" Derogatory term for a bubbly but DITZy young female. Derives from the large butterfly-like hair bows worn by such types. These became progressively more gigantic as the decade progressed, presumably as a form of arms race in competition with the increasingly **BIG HAIR** that threatened to engulf all but the most monumental accessories.

Fig. 4: Bow-Head

boy toy *noun* Either a female sex object (i.e., one regarded as a toy by a boy) or a **HIMBO** in the tow of an older woman (i.e., a boy regarded as a toy). Popularized by Madonna, who wore a "Boy Toy" belt buckle (over a wedding dress) during her performance of "Like a Virgin" at the 1984 Virgin Music Awards. *"So I'm just supposed to be your secret little boy toy?" (From "Loverboy," 1989.)*

bozack *noun* The scrotum. Phonetic variation of "ballsack." *(Ref. "Rap is Outta Control" by EPMD, 1990.)*

brah *noun* Surfer slang for "brother" or **BRO** – i.e., any male person. *"Who you, brah?" "My name's Rick." (From "North Shore," 1987.)*

brain candy *noun* Enjoyable but unchallenging entertainment, particularly in the TV sphere. See also **EYE CANDY**, **EAR CANDY**. *"I've tried to turn MAX [HEADROOM] into 'M&MTV' – brain candy." (From "Cinefantastique" magazine, 1987.)*

brain fart *noun* A momentary mental aberration, causing some thoughtless lapse or error. Also, as in the citation, an idea or thought of minimal importance or significance. *"Neither Townshend nor the Who ever threw anything away, though. They recorded every brain-fart they had." (From "Spin" magazine, 1987.)*

brainiac *noun* An intelligent person. Unlike most other such slang terms (**NERD, GEEK**, etc.) there is little or no pejorative sense (unless the term is being sarcastically applied to an evident idiot). Derives from the DC Comics supervillain and Superman adversary of the same name, a portmanteau of "brain" and "maniac." *"So what, brainiac?" (From "Ghostbusters II," 1989.)*

brain surgery *noun* See **ROCKET SCIENCE**. *"This is not a matter of life and death. It's not brain surgery. It's a game and people use it as an escape." (From "Orange Coast" magazine, October 1983.)*

brand new *adjective* A **JOCK**-y term to describe someone or something **COOL** or **FRESH**.

breakbeat *noun* A form of music or musical technique, fundamental to **HIP HOP**, utilizing the "break" of other songs as the percussion basis for new tracks. The break is the instrumental section often found in the latter half of a track, which tends to contain the most volatile drum work (as it will not be obscured by vocals). Use of these breaks in a new composition is achieved either by sampling, old-school turntable skill, or by means of special vinyl releases such as the "Ultimate Breaks and Beats" series. Perhaps the most often-sampled breakbeat, immediately recognizable from countless other tracks, is from James Brown's 1970 "Funky Drummer" (around the 5:22 mark), played by Clyde Stubblefield. See **BREAKDANCE**. *"A hip hop classic is a break beat record that everyone can use [...] Hip hop turns musical consumers into producers." (From "Bite This" by Frank Owen, "Spin" magazine, November 1989.)*

breakdance *verb* To engage in a form of energetic, athletically challenging **HIP HOP** dancing originating in the 1970s and emerging into cultural prominence in the late '70s and early '80s. The term "breakdancing" was largely a media-led modification of the original "breaking." A practitioner of the art is known as a "breaker," **B-BOY** or "B-girl." Breaking consists of four types of move: "toprock" (standing dance moves), "downrock" (floor work, often using one or more hands to support the body), "power moves" (spins and other gymnastic feats, usually performed from the floor with hands supporting the body, legs gyrating), and "freezes" (motionless poses, again usually performed from the floor and, being muscularly demanding, requiring significant strength and coordination). "Break" refers not to the likelihood of bodily injury but to the **BREAKBEAT**.

brew *noun* Beer, specifically of the ice-cold domestic pale lager variety. Key component of **ZA AND BREW**. *"I need a brew." (From "Cocoon," 1985.)*

brewski *noun* Beer; a **BREW**. Imitation Russian language, as per "Russki," etc. *"If you don't have a brewski in your hand, you might as well be wearing a dress." (From "Heathers," 1989.)*

brill *adjective* Abbreviation of "brilliant."

bringdown *noun* A saddening or sobering occurrence. Also a person whose character induces a similar effect; one whose personality test results came back negative.

bro *noun* A friend. Another **JOCK** favorite. Abbreviation of "brother" (see also **BRAH**). *"Tonight is your night, bro!" (From "Twins," 1988.)*

brody *noun* A law enforcement officer. Refers to Chief of Police Martin Brody, Roy Scheider's character in "Jaws" (1975).

brutal *adjective* Among enthusiasts of **HEAVY METAL** music, to be uncompromisingly excellent. To wield musical power with extreme skill, incisive strength, and no pretension of politeness or modesty. *"Theirs was a holy quest to become the fastest, fiercest, most brutal and punishing brotherhood on the front line of metal madness." (From "Spin" magazine, October 1988.)*

Bubba *noun* Pejorative, stereotypical term for a rural, Southern gentleman or anyone who wears bib overalls, smokes a corn cob pipe, or uses the word "chaw." *"How's yore wife, Bubba?" "Better than nothin'!" (From "The Official Rednecks [sic] Joke Book" by Larry Wilde, 1984.)*

bubble brain *noun* An idiot, fool. Synonym of **AIRHEAD**. *"In an amazing monument to bubble-brain thinking, bureaucrats [...] have squandered $35,000 for a federal grant." (From "Weekly World News," March 3, 1981.)*

bud *noun* Marijuana or a marijuana cigarette. Also a friend (from "buddy"). *(Ref. "Pothead" by Rich Kids on LSD, 1985.)*

buff *adjective* Well-toned, muscled, handsome. *"I could die. He's so buff!" (From "Valley Girl," 1983.)*

bu-fu *noun* A gay fellow. Derives from "BUtt-FUcker." See also **BOOF**. *(Ref. "Valley Girl" by Frank Zappa, 1982.)*

bug *verb* To go nuts, flip out, exhibit extremely angry, insane, or irrational behavior, or say/do something indicative of same (from "bug out"). *(Ref. "Warm It Up, Kane" by Big Daddy Kane, 1989.)*

bulk *adverb* Exceedingly ("He's bulk good"). Surf slang of Australian origin.

bummed *adjective* To be disappointed or annoyed by something. 1960s hippie slang co-opted into **VALSPEAK**. Also, more traditionally, "bummed out." *"He's got to be bummed to the max with me." (From "Valley Girl," 1983.)*

bumping *adjective* Tremendous, vibrant, jumping, swinging. *(Ref. "Paul Revere" by Beastie Boys, 1986.)*

bum-rush *verb* An unskilled frontal assault in which one seeks to overwhelm the opposition by force of numbers or weight alone. The term derives from the much earlier (1920s onward) expression "the bum's rush," (ex.: "Give him the bum's rush,") meaning the forceful ejection of a vagrant or other panhandler from a saloon. The implication was that the only time an indolent drifter would appear to rush is when being heaved aerially through a pair of batwing doors and out onto the sidewalk by two burly bouncers. Given this evolution, it is tempting to suggest that the more modern meaning implies "a rush of bums," or "an attack so simple that even bums can perform it," but there is little concrete evidence of this intention. *(Ref. 1 "Yo! Bum Rush the Show" by Public Enemy, 1987.) (Ref. 2 "Rollin' Wit' the Lench Mob" by Ice Cube, 1990.)*

bunhead *noun* A girl obsessed with ballet who due to this single-minded focus lacks other more general education or knowledge that might be expected of her; an **AIRHEAD**. Refers to a typical ballerina's habit of wearing her hair scraped up into a tight bun to keep it from flailing around and making her look like a **HEADBANGER**. *"'Has she read "Romeo and Juliet" or "Jane Eyre" or all of the Tiffany Truenote mysteries?' Zan joined in. 'No!' Rocky slammed her fist in her hand. 'That's because she's just a bunhead.'" (From "The Terrible Tryouts" – "Bad News Ballet" series #1 – by Jahnna N. Malcolm, 1989, later re-released as "Drat! We're Rats!")*

bunk *noun* Bullshit, not true, no good. From "bunkum" (originally "buncombe"), early 1800s Washington, DC slang for preposterous and meaningless political speech. *(Ref. "Square Biz" by Teena Marie, 1981.)*

buppie *noun* A young, urban, Black, affluent, professional person; a Black **YUPPIE**. *"If a buppie can be described as a professional with a college degree, living close to or in a [major] city, then I guess I'm a buppie,' says David Adams." (From "Black Enterprise" magazine, August 1985.)*

burbs *noun* Abbreviation of "suburbs": great seemingly endless tracts of uniform housing interspersed only by the occasional strip mall oasis. The suburb first achieved wide popularity in the 1950s as an attainable, comfortable option for urbanites seeking an escape from the city. Suburban life is made more complicated by the fact that streets and houses are so nearly identical as to be indistinguishable from one another. The consequent confusion of countless tired commuters arriving at the wrong houses each evening may have been responsible for the development of "swinging" in the 1960s and '70s. See also **EDGE CITY**. *"Remember what you were saying about people in the 'burbs?" (From "The 'Burbs," 1989.)*

burn! *interjection* **"buuuurn!"** Exclamation enthusiastically indicating or emphasizing that its target has been caught in a flagrant lie or gross error, or has been defeated in a battle of (half-)wits. Also "you got burned." Refers to the facial hot flush of embarrassment.

burnout *noun* A drug user, **WASTOID**, particularly one who has been mentally incapacitated to some degree by his habit. By extension, one who has been similarly debilitated by any taxing activity. *"You're breaking-in a new partner on this. [...] Real burnout, on the ragged edge." (From "Lethal Weapon," 1987.)*

bust *verb* To arrest a criminal, particularly in the act of committing a crime or with the benefit of other incontrovertible evidence. Thus, for someone in a position of authority, such as a teacher or parent, to catch one in their charge in a forbidden act, in possession of contraband, etc. In a more general sense, to catch anyone out and thus expose him or her to ridicule and humiliation. *"Ha, you got busted! Oh, that was good." (From "Planes, Trains & Automobiles," 1987.)*

bust one's balls *verb* To deliberately give someone a hard time. Also, usually when used of oneself, to expend a great deal of time and/or energy on something ("I busted my balls on this"). *"C'mon, you're breakin' my heart." "You're bustin' my balls." (From "The Dream Team," 1989.)*

butter *adjective* Very nice, slick, smooth. From "smooth as butter."

butthead *noun* An idiot, particularly an argumentative one. A pleasing semantic twofer due to the double meaning of "butt" (verb – attack with the head; noun – set of buttocks): one who has a butt for a head is likely to frequently butt heads (with other buttheads). *"Who are you calling butthead, butthead?" (From "Back to the Future Part II," 1989.)*

butt out *verb* To disengage from a conversation or other activity in which one has been meddling unhelpfully. Generally employed as an exhortative encouragement (see citation). Unrelated to "butt" as posterior, simply the reverse of "butt in" and similarly carrying the implication that the person is intruding. *"Butt out, will you? Let's talk about the preppy with the Porsche." (From "Mystic Pizza," 1988.)*

butt-ugly *adjective* Extremely unattractive. As ugly as a butt. *"Is everybody in this country as butt-ugly as you three?" (From "Quigley Down Under," 1990.)*

buzz *noun* The early or low-level effects of alcohol or narcotics. Also "buzzed" (adjective); to be under the influence to a manageable degree.

caffeinate *verb* To introduce the central nervous system stimulant caffeine into the bloodstream, usually by means of liquid refreshment. *"If you're a coffee drinker, remember this is the only cheap time to caffeinate yourself." (From "Europe Through the Back Door," by Rick Steves, 1988.)*

Calvins *noun* Underwear (of a male or female). From the ubiquitous and heavily advertised Calvin Klein brand. *"Calvins in a ball on the front seat, past eleven on a school night?" (From "The Breakfast Club," 1985.)*

camcorder *noun* A combination – both linguistically and electro-mechanically – of video camera and video tape recorder. Having revolutionized the professional market, particularly for outside TV shooting (which previously required separate camera and recording equipment) the camcorder became available to the consumer market in 1983. Typically recording to **VHS** or **BETAMAX** videotape format, recorded footage could be played back on existing home video equipment. *"Engineering sleight of hand has made JVC's new 3.3-pound VHS camcorder-player the lightest yet." (From "Popular Science" magazine, June 1986.)*

camo *adjective* Abbreviation of "camouflage." A visually disruptive pattern intended to improve concealability of equipment, vehicles, and the human form for military or hunting purposes. By extension (noun) any material imprinted with such a pattern and any clothing made from such material. *"Faded camo is no camo!" (From "Complete Bowhunting" by Glenn Helgeland, 1987.)*

candy *adjective* Descriptive of someone or something attractive or fun. *(Ref. "How Delicious She Looks" by The Buck Pets, 1989.)*

candy-ass *adjective* Sissy, effeminate, weak, unmanly. Also (noun) a person exhibiting such qualities. *"Look at you in those candy-ass monkey suits." (From "The Blues Brothers," 1980.)*

can it! *interjection* Encouragement to shut up. A popular expression in the early 20th century, declining in use from around 1920, enjoying a resurgence in the 1980s. *"You're being a wuss." "Wuss?" "Can it, Frank!" (From "The Monster Squad," 1987.)*

can you relate? *phrase* Do you understand my position? Are you able to sympathize with my emotional turmoil? The phrase has a definite touchy-feely cheesy pop psychology self-help vibe about it, so was often used for sarcastic effect (as in the lyrics of the provided citation). *(Ref. "Let's Pretend We're Married" by Prince, 1982.)*

cap *verb* To shoot (someone). Also, to insult or put down someone. Derives from "cap" (noun) idiomatically referring to a firearms cartridge or round, itself originating from pre-cartridge firearms in which the "cap" (ignition device) was separate from the "ball" (projectile). *"He's killed one terrorist for sure, and he claims he's capped off two others." (From "Die Hard," 1988.)*

caper *noun* A for-profit criminal enterprise requiring a degree of brainwork, such as a heist, con game or fraud. Crimes of passion and mundane straightforward robberies (etc.) are not capers. The standard English "caper" is a playful jump. The word derives from "capriole," from the French but also used, in English, in dressage (horse ballet – see **BUNHEAD**) to refer to an impressive but amusing four-legged jump performed by a horse while standing still, with a kick at the top. The term arrives at the slang meaning via its use to describe a practical joke or prank. The implication is that a caper, distinct from other crimes, should be not only rewarding but also lively and enjoyable and should not cause harm to those who don't have it coming to them. *"What I wouldn't give to be sitting across the table from one of the guys who pulled off that caper." (From "The A-Team" episode "A Small and Deadly War," 1983.)*

card *verb* To request the presentation of an identification card or other document claiming or implying a privilege, usually indirectly by its inclusion of a date of birth, sufficient to permit the purchase of alcohol, tobacco, or other restricted products, based on law or vendor policy. *"Two beers, please." [...] "Whoa! He didn't even card us, dude." (From "Bill & Ted's Excellent Adventure," 1989.)*

cas *adjective* **"cazh"** **VALSPEAK** abbreviation of "casual."

cassette *noun* See **TAPE**.

catch you later *phrase* Variant of "See you later." *"Great seeing you. Catch you later!" (From "Twins," 1988.)*

CD *noun* Abbreviation of "Compact Disc." A form of recorded music technology that promised to do away with the fragility and comparatively poor audio quality of vinyl records by digitally encoding music data and reading it with a laser. Originally the facts that CDs were extremely reflective and possessed a convenient hole in the center were considered secondary and irrelevant qualities. However, now that their original function has largely passed into the history books, CDs continue to be prized for these characteristics, nailed onto posts as driveway reflectors and hung on twine to scare birds away from fruit trees. *"We got everything in this mug, man. [...] CD, CB, TV, telephone, full bar, VHS." (From "Die Hard," 1988.)*

cellular *noun* Abbreviation of "cellular telephone" and precursor to "cell phone." Huge bricklike devices that resembled WWII-era military field radios, with audio quality to match. Also (adjective) in reference to any other technology related to the cellular communications network or its dependent businesses. *"Georgie! The cellular king! How you been, pal?" (From "Wall Street," 1987.)*

Fig. 5: The 1980s Cellular Telephone

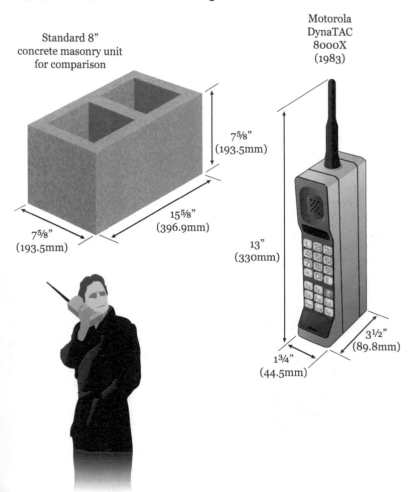

Standard 8"
concrete masonry unit
for comparison

Motorola
DynaTAC
8000X
(1983)

7⅝"
(193.5mm)

15⅝"
(396.9mm)

7⅝"
(193.5mm)

13"
(330mm)

3½"
(89.8mm)

1¾"
(44.5mm)

challenged *adjective* Of a person, to have a disability. Intended as a more polite and inclusive alternative to earlier such terms but attracting much mockery at the time, spawning amusing pseudo-hypersensitive terms such as "vertically challenged" (short).

channel surf *verb* To spend time in front of the television, cycling through programming via remote control, paying little attention to content, absorbing sense data in an uncritical state akin to hypnosis. The goal of channel surfing, like that of the activity after which it is named, is to keep going for as long as possible; to stop and actually watch one channel is a failure. See also **COUCH POTATO, VEG OUT**.

CHECK YOU LATER

"Channel surfing as a metaphor for and influence on postmodernism is, of course, not an entirely original concept." (Of course. From "Shakespearean Criticism" journal, 1984.)

check you later *phrase* Variant of "See you later." *"I'll check you later, Swede. Yeah." (From "Heartbreak Ridge," 1986.)*

cheeba *noun* Marijuana. Also "chiba." Derives from the Spanish "chiva," originally referring to heroin in South and Central America but later expanding to also mean marijuana in the early 1970s.[1] *(Ref. "Cheeba Cheeba" by Tone Loc, 1989.)*

cheese *noun* Money. Derives from the "government cheese" that was once part of welfare benefits, supplied in huge yellow-orange blocks.

cheesy *adjective* Cheap, nasty, inferior, corny, unfashionable. *(Ref. "Eat Em Up L Chill" by LL Cool J, 1990.)*

cheeuh *interjection* Spellings vary. A sort of long, drawn-out "ch-yeah" to add emphasis to whatever one is saying or express surprise, agreement, or contemptuous disbelief.

cherry *noun* One who is inexperienced at something, particularly sex. By extension (also as adjective), of an object (particularly a vehicle) to be in mint, untouched condition. *"I'm not a cherry!" "When've you ever gotten laid?" (From "The Breakfast Club," 1985.)*

chickenhawk *noun* A politician or other individual who vociferously supports sending troops to war (exhibiting hawkishness) but who himself has managed to avoid such service (being a chicken). Also "chicken hawk." One of many cheap, hard-to-swallow avian puns mocking bird-brained VP James Danforth Quayle due to his fowl surname, often parroted by those on the left wing. *"Initially, Quayle tried to duck reporters' questions regarding the hypocritical behavior of a chicken hawk." (From letter by Donald G. Westlake, "Mother Jones" magazine, December 1988.)*

chill *verb* To relax, take it easy, cool down. To do nothing, but with panache. Relaxing was big in the 1980s, partly due to the general emphasis on being **COOL**, but also thanks to Frankie Goes to Hollywood's giant 1984 hit "Relax." Commonly used as an exhortation. Also, adjectively ("chilling"), a contronym[2] – "frightening." *"Break it up!" "Come on, Elias, chill!" (From "Platoon," 1986.)*

chill out *verb* Elongation of **CHILL**. Often said with emphasis on the second word, to indicate a growing irritation with whatever the person is being un**COOL** about. *"I gotta drive, Slug! I gotta drive!" "Alright already, alright! Will you chill out?" (From "The Toxic Avenger," 1985.)*

chill pill *noun* An imaginary tranquilizer.

Chinese fire drill *noun* Generally, a state of total confusion, frenetic activity and panic, achieving nothing, particularly if this is due to the meaning of instructions becoming lost in translation. Specifically, a college prank in which the occupants of an automobile, stationary at

---

1. According to "A Marihuana Dictionary," by Ernest L. Abel, 1982.
2. An auto-antonym; a word that means its own opposite.

a red light, jump out of the car, frantically run round it, and reenter to take a different seat before the light turns green. The phrase is now considered objectionable by some. *[After some extremely confused dialog.]* *"Mr. HYDE: This is like a Chinese fire drill." (From "Martial Law on Taiwan and United States Foreign Policy Interests: Hearing Before the Subcommittee on Asian and Pacific Affairs of the Committee on Foreign Affairs, House of Representatives," May 20, 1982.)*

chiseled *adjective* To have sharp, clean lines, as of a Greek statue. Of muscles, particularly abs, to be well defined. One who is chiseled certainly has a low body fat percentage but is not as drastically lean as one who is **RIPPED**. *"Exercise Breakthrough! Electro Training – Produce Huge Muscular Peaks and Chiseled Definition." (From mail order advertisement in "Black Belt" magazine, November 1985.)*

chocoholic *noun* A recreational abuser of chocolate.

choice *adjective, interjection* Exquisite, the pick of the bunch, as in "a choice morsel." That which one would choose. As an interjection, simply "excellent."

chonies *noun* Underpants. From the Spanish "calzones" (breeches) or possibly the similar Italian "calzoni" (from which we get the "calzone" folded pizza, due to its arguable resemblance to a trouser leg).

chopper *noun* A helicopter, due to the action of the rotor blades through the air, or a "chopped" (modified; cut and elongated) motorcycle. Also a practitioner of a style of rap emphasizing fast, machine-gun vocal delivery, from the (originally Jamaican) street slang for an AK-47 or other full auto weapon. *"Get to the chopper!" (From "Predator," 1987.)*

chrome-plated *adjective* Well-dressed, particularly of a woman. Originally 1960s hot-rodder slang, based on the obvious association with a "dressed-up" piece of automobile bodywork.

chud *noun* A repulsive, nauseating person. Refers to the titular antagonists of the 1984 cult classic subterranean horror movie "C.H.U.D." (Cannibalistic Humanoid Underground Dwellers), in which unfortunate homeless inhabitants of a grimy New York slum are dragged away, killed, and eaten by once-human, radioactive, tunnel-dwelling **MUTANT**s. The movie was seen by some as an allegory for gentrification (see **YUPPIFY**).

chug *verb* To consume a beverage, usually a **BREW**, in a single action without pause for breath. Abbreviation of the older (1940s) slang "chugalug." *"If the accusation is correct, the 'killer' must chug a beer for every player left alive." (from "The Complete Book of Beer Drinking Games (and Other Really Important Stuff)" by Griscom, Rand and Johnston, 1989.)*

clock *verb* To whack someone or something hard, particularly if the victim didn't see it coming. From the phrase "clean (one's) clock." Also, to earn money. Also "clocker," a crack dealer: the drug's addictive potential would require an attentive distributor to be on call around the clock. *"I said, 'I ain't punching nobody.' My ego said, 'Well, gimme your hand.' Clocked that boy in his eye." (From "Eddie Murphy Raw," 1987.)*

Club Fed *noun* Federal prison, operated by the Federal Bureau of Prisons for the corrective benefit of those who have been convicted of violating US federal law. A humorous allusion to the well-known and heavily-advertised Club Med company, specializing in all-inclusive luxurious resort vacations. *"Federal Prison Camp – better known as 'Club Fed' for its cushy accommodations and prominent guest list – may get some lower-class neighbors before long." (From "Southern Exposure" journal, by the Institute for Southern Studies, 1989.)*

club kid *noun* An overenthusiastic habitual inhabitant of the night-club scene, particularly in New York, in eternal pursuit of glamour and intoxication as art. *"The ever-contradictory Claude Montana will not attend the last event. 'I was a club kid,' he says. 'I still am.' [...] 'I should maybe be less a club kid. I need to be more calm.'" (From "New York" magazine, July 31, 1989.)*

clutch *adjective* Cool – particularly when involving some skill or luck, but also in a more general sense. Derives from term's use in sport to refer to a team or athlete's ability to deliver superlative performance under pressure or "in the clutch," resulting in a "clutch play."

Clydesdale *noun* An approving term used by girls to refer to a muscular, handsome, physically capable male specimen. Derives from the Clydesdale horse breed, a particularly impressive beast from Scotland employed in the locomotion of heavy loads such as beer wagons. The Clydesdale horse also tends to have a pleasant, long-suffering and helpful demeanor, so the term's use to describe a person avoids the connotation of violence or stupidity present in other less positive terms (i.e., "meathead," "lunk," JOCK, "muscle-bound oaf," etc.)

coals *noun* Cigarette or other smokable. Derives from the burning tip of such.

coast *verb* To relax and take it easy. As of a vehicle continuing to move at speed without additional mechanical effort, in neutral gear or with the clutch depressed, due to momentum and/or gradient. *"If Ferris thinks that he can just coast through this month and still graduate, he is sorely mistaken." (From "Ferris Bueller's Day Off," 1986.)*

coaster *noun* Descriptive but nonetheless derogatory VALSPEAK term for one who lives on the coast and whose standards of dress and behavior have consequently devolved. A beach bum; the sort of person who necessitates "No shirt, no shoes, no service" signs.

cock diesel *adjective* Strong, muscular, either literally or figuratively. Negatively, muscle-bound. See also DIESEL. *(Ref. "Who Am I?" by Big Daddy Kane and Gamilah Shabazz, 1990.)*

cocoon *verb* To remain comfortably at home in preference to going out. By extension ("cocooning"), the act of setting up one's home in a comfortable and pleasant manner in preparation for so doing. Coined in 1981 by marketing consultant Faith Popcorn[1] to define a trend away from potentially dangerous (or, at least, tiring) socia

---

1. Née Plotkin.

interaction. The expectation was that this would drive consumer spending on safe, domestic, reassuring products and activities. *"The harassments of daily life – looming nuclear incineration, rude waiters – have driven people to 'cocooning.' They have gone to ground in their dens with their VCRs and compact-disc players." (From "Of Consuming Interest," by George F. Will, "Washington Post," June 11, 1987.)*

coin *noun* Money. Also in the plural, "coins." *"We'll win some serious coin, right?" (From "Uncle Buck," 1989.)*

Coke-bottle glasses *noun* Unattractive and unfashionable eyeglasses with lenses so thick they resemble the bases of Coca-Cola bottles. Similar in effect to the "BCGs" (Birth Control Glasses) issued to members of the US armed forces, so named due to their elimination of any chance the wearer might have of getting anywhere near a member of the opposite sex. *"Alan 'Blind Owl' Wilson [...] was a nearsighted young man with Coke-bottle glasses and an inclination toward scholarly pursuits in the blues field." (From "Spin" magazine, April 1986.)*

cold *adjective* Ruthless, without feeling ("cold-blooded"). Also descriptive of an especially attractive woman of the aloof, seemingly unattainable type. *"I'm driving, I've seen your car." "Oh, shit, that's cold." (From "Beverly Hills Cop," 1984.)*

cold lamping *noun* CHILLing out, relaxing. Origin obscure, but popularized by the cited Public Enemy track. *(Ref. "Cold Lampin' With Flavor," by Public Enemy, 1988.)*

Commodore *noun* A product of Commodore Business Machines (CBM), manufacturer of the finest personal computers of the 1980s, the Commodore 64, 128, and Amiga series. *[Notices bowling ball embedded in crushed home computer.] "They said the Commodore would stand up to anything!" (From "Earth Girls are Easy," 1989.)*

conehead *noun* One who is unfamiliar with the ways of this planet and is thus liable to make elementary errors (see also **ZOD**). A **WEIRDO**. Derives from the Saturday Night Live "Coneheads" sketch dating from 1977, featuring Dan Aykroyd and Jane Curtin, and Frank Zappa's 1981 song "Conehead." *"Only a grade-A conehead would've thought that way." (From "The Gold Flake Hydrant" by Greg Matthews, 1988.)*

cool *adjective* A zen-like state of being yearningly desired by many, paradoxically achievable only by those who have ceased to care about it or who possess it innately. One who is cool exists without apparently exerting effort in any direction, but nonetheless unerringly achieves success in any endeavor simply by virtue of a sympathetic harmonic vibration in tune with the universal frequency. Or, at least, by working incredibly hard when no one's watching. In the 1980s the concept of "cool" was formalized in religious dogma by the Church of the Subgenius, a controversial Dallas-based for-profit ecclesiastical outfit, in the term "slack." This refers to an ultimately desirable but intangible commodity definable only by each individual, which enables its possessor to accomplish great feats by "surfing the luck plane." In a more general sense,

COOL BEANS

"good." *"Too cool, too cool! Very cool! Very, very cool! Yes!" (From "Stand by Me," 1986.)*

cool beans *interjection* Good, excellent. The phrase may be related to the old saying "some beans," meaning "quite something," and to the general use of beans in various expressions, such as "Give 'er the beans!" (accelerate hard). The phrase gained popularity from its use in the TV situation comedy "Full House."

cool out *verb* To take it easy, calm down, take a **CHILL PILL.** *"I know you have domestic troubles. But you got to cool out, relax." (From "Beverly Hills Cop II," 1987.)*

cooze *noun* The female genitalia. Dates back to the 1920s, but a common choice of vocabulary in the 1980s, particularly when use of a more reprehensible synonym would be unwarranted or, in movies, frowned upon by the Motion Picture Association. *"Brad's saying you're being a real cooze." (From "Heathers," 1989.)*

copy *verb* As a question ("Copy?") to tersely inquire whether the listener has heard and understood what one just said. As a statement ("Copy!") to succinctly affirm that one has indeed gotten the message. Military radio protocol that found its way into the mainstream via movie usage. *"This is blue leader to blue bikes. Run these guys into your jet walls. Copy, blue leader." "Copy, blue leader." (From "Tron," 1982.)*

couch potato *noun* Lumpy, roughly ovoid, motionless vegetable matter found on living room furniture, entranced by the idiot box: a television addict. Rarely encountered today, having been largely supplanted by the YouTuber. 1983's popular "The Official Couch Potato Handbook" ("A Guide to Prolonged Television Viewing") described itself as celebrating "The Recline of Western Civilization." See also **VEG OUT.** *"You lose IQ points the longer you watch. [...] Look, you're going to become the first alien couch potato." (From "Short Circuit," 1986.)*

cowabunga *interjection* An expression of wild exuberance or exhilaration, often issued on beginning some dangerous or otherwise ill-advised action, like "Geronimo!" The exact origin of this term is unknown, but it was used as a catchphrase by Chief Thunderthud on the 1950s TV show "Howdy Doody," as "cowabonga." Thunderthud's song "Cowabonga" (with Mitch Miller and Orchestra, 1955) encouraged listeners to use the word in various exasperating situations as a way of keeping calm. It was later adopted by surfers then popularized by surfer-imitators and the Teenage Mutant Ninja Turtles in the late '80s, followed by Bart Simpson. *"Cowabunga: The snow looks great, let's hit the slopes!'" (From "Board Talk" article on the newly popular snowboarding sport and its surf/skateboard-derived language, "Skiing magazine, October 1988.)*

coyote date *noun* An unappealing romantic partner; same derivation as **COYOTE UGLY.** *"You see policemen with coyote dates. [...] Who do you think a guy meets in topless bars and strip joints and hooker bars?" (From "Cops by Mark Baker, 1989.)*

coyote ugly *adjective* Terrifyingly unattractive. Derivation as in the citation (coyotes are famous for doing this to escape traps). The phrase does not imply that coyotes are themselves ugly. *"Coyote ugly is when you wake up next to a woman so ugly that you chew your arm off to get out of there without waking her up." (From "Bad Fortune" by Daniel Lynch, 1989.)*

cracked out *adjective* Descriptive of the wretched and incompetent state of the long-term crack cocaine user and therefore applicable to any boneheaded or mush-minded ("compost mentis") individual.

crackhead *noun* A habitual user of crack cocaine, or someone whose actions or thoughts are sufficiently dysfunctional to mimic the deleterious effects of the drug. *"Every night, wide-eyed, gold-bedecked teenage crackheads do 75 miles an hour on the Henry Hudson Parkway, racing one another in BMWs." (from "New York" magazine, August 1988.)*

crack, on *adjective* One side effect of the 1980s crack cocaine epidemic (see **BASE**) was that the originator of any spectacularly imbecilic thought, opinion, or behavior would be likely to receive a response politely but incredulously wondering whether he/she was a user of the drug: "Are you on crack?"

cranking *adjective* Highly energetic, wild. **VALSPEAK** derived from surf slang. *"Hey, listen. Waimea's cranking right now. We're just goin' out." (From "North Shore," 1987.)*

creep out *verb* To make someone feel uneasy by means of inappropriate or disquietingly eerie behavior; to "give them the creeps." "Creep" has been used in this sense since the fourteenth century, synonymously with "crawl" (as in "it made my skin crawl"). *"This whole situation is creeping me out." (From "Touring with the Alien" by Carolyn Ives Gilman, appearing in "The Year's Best Science Fiction: Fifth Annual Collection," 1988.)*

crib *noun* A domicile: house, apartment, etc. *(Ref. "Jungle Love" by Morris Day and The Time, 1984.)*

Croakies *noun* A type of retainer strap for sunglasses, made of neoprene, often brightly colored. Prevents loss of the glasses and allows them to be worn around the neck when not in use. Very **PREPPY**-on-spring-break. See **SHADES**. *"Croakies keep a grip on your glasses so you don't have to." (From "Croakies" advertisement, "Skiing" magazine, December 1983.)*

crucial *adjective* Extremely good. Derives from the word's standard definition as something fundamental or critical but used in a looser sense. *(Ref. "Adore" by Prince, 1987.)*

crudball *noun* A dirty or off-putting person. Slightly less insulting synonym of "dirtball" and often used jokingly, as in the citation. *"Listen, crudball, we'll have an amazing Christmas, okay?" (From "Two & Two Together" by Julia Whedon, 1983.)*

cruft *noun* Unidentifiable but unpleasant stuff, particularly waste material that builds up over time. In computing, functional but wasteful and inefficient code. *"CRUFTY [...] yucky, like spilled coffee smeared with peanut butter and catsup. [...] Poorly built, possibly overly complex." (From "The Hacker's Dictionary," 1983 edition.)*

cruisemobile *noun* A **COOL**, desirable automobile. Not necessarily a high-performance car, but not a **HOOPTIE**, either. *"Like if you're* *impressed, you go, 'Wo, man, like cruisemobile, huh,' or something." (From "Adolescence, Adolescents," by Barbara Schneider Fuhrmann, 1990.)*

crunchy *adjective* Jealous. Etymology uncertain, but possibly related to the bruxism (gnashing of teeth) of an uncontrollably envious person. Alternatively, associated with hippie culture, referencing the texture of granola bars (see **GRANOLA-EATER**) and the results of neglected bodily hygiene.

crusty *adjective* Dirty, low-rent, grimy.

cut to the chase *phrase* Get to the point. Refers to the desire, when watching a movie, to move directly to the next car chase scene rather than having to suffer through more tedious dialog, lumpy character development, clumsy narrative exposition, etc. *"So what do you say we cut to the chase?" (From "Wall Street," 1987.)*

cyberpunk *noun* See **PUNK**.

dag *interjection* Exclamation of surprise. A modification ("taboo deformation" or "minced oath") of "damn," likely via "doggone"/"daggone," and used in an identical way. *(Ref. "Brainwashed Follower" by De La Soul, 1989.)*

damage *noun* Malfunction causing a person to behave in an unwelcome manner. Almost always used in inquiry; see **WHAT'S YOUR DAMAGE?** *"What's your damage? Brad's saying you're being a real cooze." (From "Heathers," 1989.)*

damn Sam *interjection* Rhyming exclamation of surprise, annoyance, etc. *[Calling bingo] "'B,' as in 'Bathsheba,' fourteen." "Bingo!" "Damn Sam!" (From the "M*A*S*H" episode "The Moon is Not Blue," December 13, 1982.)*

damn skippy *interjection* Affirmative exclamation. "You bet," "damn right." *"Is that all you guys think about? Is that it?" "You damn skippy." (From "School Daze," 1988.)*

dank *adjective* Excellent, high-quality. Possibly simply an example of vernacular "meaning inversion" (or "amelioration" – "bad," "wicked," etc.) due to its original definition (unpleasantly moist, humid, and odorous) or possibly due to an association with **PRIMO** marijuana.

d-bag *noun* Abbreviation of **DOUCHEBAG**.

deadly *adjective* Cool, excellent, stylish, or skillful. Often used to inflict biting but unprovable sarcasm due both to its hyperbole and its somewhat ambiguous meaning ("deadly dull," etc.) *(Ref. "Pamela" by Toto, 1988.)*

dead meat *noun* One who is inescapably doomed. *"You lose concentration in a fight and you're dead meat." (From "The Karate Kid," 1984.)*

decaf *noun* Abbreviation of "decaffeinated coffee." Coffee from which the caffeine has been removed via an industrial process involving solution and osmosis. Popularized in the late 1970s and early '80s and consumed by people who, presumably having gotten away with serious crimes in the past, felt the guilty psychological need to self-punish. See also **MOCKTAIL**.

decent *adjective* Good, cool. Not necessarily awesome, but solid, dependable, high-quality. *"What a decent night, huh?" (From "Sixteen Candles," 1984.)*

deck *verb* To punch someone or beat them up; to make them hit the deck. *"Laugh and I'll deck you." (From "Pretty in Pink," 1986.)*

deep shit *noun* The substance in which one is immersed when in trouble, danger, or some other dire predicament. *"At least we know where we stand." "Yeah. In deep shit." (From "Big Trouble in Little China," 1986.)*

def *adjective* Originally (adverb) simply a contraction of "definitely," later "cool," "stylish" or "exquisite." *"Is that all you're into? 'Good hair, def body.'" (From "House Party," 1990).*

deke *verb* To fake someone out, fool them, or trick them out of something. From "decoy" in a sporting sense.

designer drug *noun* A lab-created recreational pharmaceutical, as opposed to a naturally derived one such as marijuana, cocaine, or heroin. The term was coined to describe various synthetic heroin analogs created to solve the "problems" associated with traditional methods of sourcing and importing narcotics, but soon came to refer to new "party drugs" such as MDMA (see **ECSTASY**). Semiotically, use of the term "designer," though explicitly referring to the man-made nature of the substances, lent a certain unintentional positive sense to the phrase; the listener would naturally associate it with the contemporaneous colloquialisms for fashionable, desirable looks and clothing, such as **DESIGNER JEANS** and **DESIGNER STUBBLE**. *"What is even more alarming is the growth of underground chemical labs which produce 'designer drugs' – chemical analogs of heroin and cocaine which mimic the drugs' effects but cannot be detected in the body and are legal to manufacture." (From "Boca Raton News," April 4, 1985.)*

designer jeans *noun* While denim jeans had been unassailably fashionable for several decades, until the 1980s the rationale for this stylishness was that they were repurposed workwear: classic, hard-wearing, no-nonsense, iconic Americana. Their wearers were **COOL**, according to the marketing departments of Levis, Wrangler, and others, precisely because they were people of simple good taste who appreciated tried and tested classics and definitely not the sort of try-hard fashionista types who cared about this year's designs or dubious European-sounding labels (see **EUROFAG**). All this changed beginning in the mid–late 1970s, and the traditionalists were overwhelmed by the 1980s. Despite the resurgence of the 1950s/'60s blue jeans and white T-shirt aesthetic, labels like Calvin Klein, Jordache, Guess, and Gloria Vanderbilt dazzled the public with a bewildering variety of colors, fits, washes, materials, and embellishments. Following the trend for ever more extremely pre-distressed designer denim, by 1990 one company was offering jeans and jean jackets taken to the range and peppered with buckshot and birdshot sold under the trademark "Shotgun Wash." *"The slightest peep and your designer jeans ain't gonna fit no more." (From "Beverly Hills Cop II," 1987.)*

designer stubble *noun* A deliberately unshaven style for men, with a beard of (typically) one to two days' growth, signifying a nonchalant, carefree outlook, popularized by Don Johnson of the TV show "Miami Vice" and George Michael of the pop group "Wham!" in the early 1980s. The appropriate beard-hair length of around two to three millimeters is sufficient to give the wearer the required insouciant appearance, but not long enough to look messy (which fo the average man might happen on the third or fourth day). However, shaving would cause one to lose the look completely and necessitate staying hidden from public view until it had grown back, severely cramping one's style. Therefore, electric beard trimmers soon emerged that trimmed the hair an appropriate length from the skin and thus enabled the stubble-wearer to maintain his image indefinitely. The cultivation of designer stubble does not mean that the wearer does not shave daily; many aficionados prefer a clean razor line around the stubble, particularly at the neck line but also atop the lower mandible in order to accentuate cheekbone definition. The word "designer" in this case is adopted due to the intentional, image-focused adoption of the stubble, as well as its association with the fashion world, male models, and stylish celebrities. *"After all, everything is 'designed' and the way the word is now used, to mean visual quality and style, has become so overused that we now have designer cars and even designer stubble." (From "Engineering Materials and Design: EM&D" journal, vol. 33, 1989.)*

dexter *noun* A bookish, studious, socially and stylistically inept, overly cautious, un**COOL**, boring person. The term derives from "Poindexter," a character from the old "Felix the Cat" cartoon, later reused for the character Arnold Poindexter from "Revenge of the **NERD**s" (1984).

dick *noun* A male organ. Also an insult for any egotistical, thoughtless person, roughly synonymous with **JERK**. Often combined with other bodily specifics for emphasis or metaphoric variety: "dickhead," "dickbrain," "dickface," "dick-fingered" (clumsy), and so on and so forth. *"Yee-hah! Just like fucking Saigon, eh, Slick?" "I was in Junior High, dickhead." (From "Die Hard," 1988.)*

dickweed *noun* Elaboration of **DICK**. An obnoxious individual. Possibly an allusion to pubic hair or just undesirable vegetation. A perennial favorite insult on "Mystery Science Theater 3000" (first aired in 1988). *"You killed Ted, you medieval dickweed!" (From "Bill & Ted's Excellent Adventure," 1989.)*

diesel *adjective* Excellent, cool, powerful. Alludes to the fact that diesel engines are typically the power plant of choice for large, mighty vehicles, due to their capacity for high torque output at low RPMs. See also **COCK DIESEL**. *(Ref. "Big Shots" by King Sun, 1990.)*

dinero *noun* Cash money. *"Who's got the beaucoup dolares today?" "Uno dinero." (From "Fast Times at Ridgemont High," 1982.)*

DINK *noun* Acronym. A member of a married, childless couple with both partners in paid employment – "Double (or Dual) Income, No Kids." Such an individual is presumed to possess significant amounts of disposable income and free time, thus attracting the envy of their progeny-blessed friends. Also "DINKY" – "Double Income, No Kids Yet." See also **YUPPIE**. Also (unrelated, lowercase) an idiot. *"The so-called yuppie generation [...] has now been supplanted by DINKs – that is, double income/no kids. [Laughter]" (Statement of Hon. Loret M. Ruppe, Director, Peace Corps, to the US Senate, Subcommittee on Western Hemisphere and Peace Corps*

DINO-RHINO

Affairs of the Committee on Foreign Relations, Washington, DC, Thursday, March 26, 1987.)

dino-rhino *adjective* Cool, awesome. Origin unclear, but possibly simply a rhyming elongation of **DYNO** or in consideration of the awe-inspiring aspects of dinosaurs and rhinoceroses. *"[Teens] even use a vocabulary which is not meant to be understood by anyone outside of the group. Some 'tribal membership' teen lingo which was overheard recently included: [...] punk, freaks, awesome, this dude is dino-rhino, grits, hosers, slime and scuzz." (From T.E.A.M., the Early Adolescence Magazine, Volume 1, 1986.)*

dip *verb* To eavesdrop on a conversation.

dipshit *noun* All-purpose, highly satisfying insult. Essentially an asinine, inept, naive, malcoordinated, feckless, clumsy, inconsequential person, but more or less justifiably applicable to any person at any time and possessing very robust grammatical flexibility (see citation). Often used affectionately. *"Goddamn dipshit Rodriguez gypsy dildo punks!" (From "Repo Man," 1984.)*

dipstick *noun* A blockhead. Family-friendly version of **DIPSHIT**. Derives from the long strip of metal used in an automobile engine to gauge the quantity of lubricating oil in circulation. *"If that dipstick deputy of yours don't win that race for me, I'm gonna skin him alive and have me the ugliest throw rug in Hazzard County." (From "The Dukes of Hazzard" episode "Luke's Love Story," 1979.)*

dirt nap *noun* Earthy euphemism for death, the big sleep. *"You would have been face to face with starvation, and the prospect of taking a dirt nap." (From "Field and Stream" magazine, 1989.)*

dirty laundry *noun* Potentially embarrassing personal, family, or business issues, which should be dealt with in private, not displayed in public. *"I don't think we should be airing our dirty laundry in front of the neighbors." (From the "ALF" episode "Lookin' Through the Windows," 1987.)*

dis *verb* To disrespect, disparage, dishonor or do a discouraging discourtesy unto another. Sometimes spelled "diss." Also as a noun: "He didn't mean it as a dis." *"Dude, where'd she dump you, man?" "In a car." "Your car?" "Aw, man! Dissed in the Malibu?" (From "Say Anything...," 1989.)*

disco *noun* Mainstream musical fad of the 1970s centered around dance clubs or "discotheques." So thoroughly reviled for its elitist plasticity that the explosive, purgative anti-disco counterrevolution was powerful enough to result in the creation of new musical genres with sufficient momentum to define the entire decade of the 1980s: **PUNK**, **NEW WAVE**, and **HIP HOP**. The symbolic watershed moment that set the stage for the shiny new cultural order was the "Disco Demolition Night" of July 12th, 1979, at Comiskey Park baseball stadium, Chicago. At the event, militant anti-disco activist and rock DJ Steve Dahl offered discounted entry for attendees surrendering sacrificial disco records, which were placed in a large crate in center field and ceremonially destroyed with explosives. The display attracted over fifty thousand people, many of whom stormed the gates and filled the park far beyond capacity. After the cathartic detonation, ecstatic fans – drunk on victory and Miller Lite – rushed the now badly-cratered field in celebration, setting fires and battling police in a running riot.[1] The evening became one of the most memorable but, depending on perspective, least successful promotional events in Major League Baseball history. *"The first thing is, Jules, forget about disco. Right?" "No disco?" "No disco." (From "Twins," 1988.)*

ditz *noun* An **AIRHEAD**, usually female. The term implies forgetfulness, confusion, and generally not knowing which planet one is currently orbiting around. *"Hi, can you help me? I'm such a ditz. I left my tennis racket in one of your cabs today." (from "Outrageous Fortune," 1987.)*

do lunch *verb* A **YUPPIE** classic. To have lunch with someone; possibly even a **POWER LUNCH** if you're lucky. Often used (as in the citation) as a reasonably polite way of terminating an unwelcome encounter with a vague suggestion of future engagement. *"They tried to smother him. His tubes got all pulled out." "Yeah, listen, I got a ten o'clock at Bristol. Nice meeting you all. We gotta do lunch, Jack." (From "The Dream Team," 1989.)*

don't have a cow *phrase* Relax, take a **CHILL PILL**, quit freaking out. In medieval times various superstitions existed relating to the concern that women might give birth to kittens rather than a human child, giving us the phrase "to have kittens," meaning to exhibit an extremely negative emotional reaction. One therefore assumes that while having kittens would certainly be distressing, to have an entire cow would be likely to result in a whole new level of concern. While the phrase has more recently become indelibly associated with Bart Simpson, as far back as 1926 Gertrude Stein wrote a book with the improbable title "A Book Concluding with As a Wife Has a Cow: A Love Story." The phrase's longevity is therefore perhaps related to the striking mental image it unavoidably produces in the hearer. See also **SHITTING BRICKS**. *"I'm getting strange signals." "Well they're not coming from me. Everything's fine, don't have a cow." (From "Sixteen Candles," 1984.)*

doobie *noun* A marijuana cigarette. Also "doobage," meaning marijuana in general. *"Can I have my doobage?" (From "The Breakfast Club," 1985.)*

doofus *noun* An idiot, a dunderhead. Someone you wouldn't trust to sit the right way round on a toilet. Also "dufus." *"We've got to find poor Michelangelo, too!" "Don't be a doofus, babe. I'm right here." (From the "Cowabunga Shredhead" episode of "Teenage Mutant Ninja Turtles," 1989.)*

dope *adjective* Good, cool, hip. Also (noun) marijuana or, in some circumstances, another drug. *(Ref. "Doper than Dope" by Salt-N-Pepa, 1990.)*

dork *noun* Originally a penis. Later, any person exhibiting implied characteristics of that organ. An un**COOL**, awkward type; in particular, one whose clothing and possessions are unfashionable or substandard. *"Hey, Biff, get a load of this guy's life preserver! Dork thinks he's going to drown." (From "Back to the Future," 1985.)*

---

1. The chaos was so tumultuous that "The Green Mile" actor Michael Clarke Duncan, then twenty-one years old, discovered his belt buckle had been stolen in the free-for-all. In 2006, Duncan proudly told the Chicago Sun-Times, "It was death to disco that night. I am part of history."

do the nasty *verb* To have sex, **BOINK**. *"I can't be staying long." "How long?" "Long enough to do the nasty." (From "Do the Right Thing," 1989.)*

do the wild thing *verb* "do the wild thaang" To **DO THE NASTY**, **BOINK**. *(Ref. "Wild Thing" by Tone Loc, 1989.)*

douchebag *noun* A feminine hygiene product; also a contemptible person. While use of this term reached its zenith in the 1980s, it was recorded as an insult as far back as the '50s.

downsize *verb* Of a corporation, to lay off staff, often to the displeasure of **YUPPIES**. *"They invested twenty billion dollars in downsizing between 1974 and 1980." (From "The New Yorker" magazine, April 28 1980.)*

down with *phrase* To be in a state of acceptance, agreement, understanding, or approval ("I'm down with that"). Also simply "I'm down," (meaning "Count me in"). By extension, when used of a person or group, to be friends, allied, or at least simpatico with the named party. *(Ref. "I Got the Knack" by Everlast, 1990.)*

doy *interjection* Interjection expressing the thought that one's conversational partner has said something blindingly obvious or foolish. Also "d'oi," "doi," "duh," "dur," etc. "No doy" is essentially equivalent to **NO SHIT, SHERLOCK**. Though ubiquitous in its various forms throughout the 1980s, the expression was used much less in the early 1990s (as remarked upon in the citation), perhaps due to a growing perception that it might be seen as mocking the afflicted. See also **DUH**. *"All right, when did you have it on last?" "Doy! Probably right before she lost it." "You don't get a lot of 'doy' these days." (From the "Friends" episode "The One with the Sonogram at the End," September 29, 1994.)*

drain the lizard *verb* Of a male, to urinate; take a leak. *"Hey, troops! Had to drain the lizard." (from "Earth Girls are Easy," 1988.)*

drop science *verb* To impart knowledge, educate: to place wisdom in front of the listener. As noted in the citation's lyrics, the meaning is something of a contronym ("drop science" also meaning to quit that class at school and thus remain ignorant). *(Ref. "You Played Yourself" by Ice-T, 1989.)*

druggies *noun* A common high school clique: **BURNOUT**s, dropouts, **WASTOID**s. Adherents of the group may or may not actually consume illicit narcotics but nonetheless certainly work hard to create that impression.

duckets *noun* Money. The "ducat" was a European gold or silver coin originating in the Late Middle Ages. The term found its way into modern slang via Shakespeare (see **NICE PLAY, SHAKESPEARE**), who uses it profusely (at least thirty times in "The Merchant of Venice" alone): "Dead, for a ducat, dead!" *(Ref. "You Played Yourself" by Ice-T, 1989)*

dude *noun* The quintessential 1980s word, which not only remains in extremely popular use but also has much older roots. "Dude," a pejorative meaning "dandy" (a well-dressed but flamboyant gentleman) dates back a century to the 1880s. Socialite and sartorially splendid man-about-town Evander Berry Wall was crowned "King of the

Dudes" back in 1883. Wall famously once changed clothes forty times between breakfast and dinner. In the early twentieth century, the term did duty in the phrase "dude ranch" – a tourist ranch, run for those feeling nostalgic for the Old West. Again there was a depreciatory connotation; that those who vacationed there were urbanite sissies (an attitude that persisted, being the central joke of the 1991 movie "City Slickers"). In the years since, the term has become more of a catchall title for the everyman. In 1969's "Easy Rider," Peter Fonda's character Wyatt says, "'Dude' means a nice guy, you know? 'Dude' means a regular sort of person." In the 1980s, both senses persisted – though now with no negative connotation at all. An average Joe was a "regular dude," and a slick, snappy dresser with **ATTITUDE** was a "**COOL** dude" (**SHADES** mandatory). Still in use, though not as popular as his '80s heyday, the dude remains with us through the centuries; he abides. *(Ref. "This is the Life" by "Weird Al" Yankovic, 1985.)*

dudette *noun* A female **DUDE**. *"Hey, I miss you, dude." "I miss you too, dudette." (From the "Miami Vice" episode "Theresa," 1987.)*

dudical *adjective* Exhibiting the qualities of a **DUDE**; **AWESOME**, **COOL**. A portmanteau of "dude" and **RADICAL**. *"'The new word is "dudical,"' Walt says. 'I learned it from my kids. It means "really cool," like when a radical dude does something awesome.'" (From "What We're Up To" by Gil Schwartz, New York Magazine, July 17, 1989).*

dudley / dudly *noun* An unexciting, humdrum male of no conceivable romantic interest. Possibly derives from Dudley Do-Right, the boringly good Mountie from "The Rocky and Bullwinkle Show," or from "dud" + "ly"; one who fails to be useful, effective, or successful. Either way, a pleasing rhyming antonym to "studly."

duh *interjection* "**duh / du-uh / du-uh-uh / du-uh-uh-uh**" Expression mimicking slack-jawed imbecility (see **MOUTH-BREATHER**) employed sarcastically in response to hearing something incredibly obvious or stupid, or in self-rebuke (as in the citation). Emphasis and repetition of the "uh" (see pronunciation) increases the severity of the condemnation. Also "no duh," in response to an obviosity, synonymously with **NO SHIT, SHERLOCK**. See also **DOY**. *"I guess you know why I called you in here." "Uh, because you're lonely?" "No, you moron." "Oh, duh." (From "UHF," 1989.)*

dweeb *noun* An inadequate, weedy, weak, and socially inept person: a nebbish. Possibly possessing a glimmer of intelligence or academic ability, but probably a sad bumbler in that area as in every other; a wannabe **NERD**. Also a larger, chewier, softer and, appropriately, less successful version of the "Nerds" candy, introduced in the early '90s and discontinued shortly thereafter. *"The sportos, the motorheads, geeks, sluts, bloods, wastoids, dweebies, dickheads – they all adore him." (From "Ferris Bueller's Day Off," 1986.)*

dyno *adjective* Cool, great, high-energy, explosively and excitingly awesome. Abbreviation of "dynamite." *"I'll tell you one thing, unless your project is dyno-supreme, you both get Ds" (From "My Science Project," 1985.)*

ear candy *noun* A piece of enjoyable but lightweight music. See also **EYE CANDY, BRAIN CANDY**. *"Cuts like the title track [...] are the sure-fire ear candy he's grown adept at churning out." (From "The Atlantic" magazine, 1987.)*

eat me *interjection* Exclamation of dismissive, derisive disagreement or in response to an insult. See also **BITE ME**. *"If someone comes up to with an attitude you say 'eat me.'" (From "Terminator 2," 1991.)*

eat my shorts *interjection* Defiant or contemptuous exclamation, equivalent to "go pound sand," "get lost," "go piss up a rope," etc. *(Ref. "Eat My Shorts" by Rick Dees, 1984.)*

ecstasy *noun* The synthetic **DESIGNER DRUG** 3,4-Methylene-dioxymethamphetamine (MDMA). MDMA had been used in certain psychiatric therapies and emerged into wider recreational use in the late 1970s through word-of-mouth networks. Ecstasy became associated with the nightclub and **DISCO** scenes in several American cities and in the early to mid-1980s it could be purchased by credit card from toll-free phone numbers. The drug was made illegal in the US in 1985. Despite or because of this, ecstasy soon became indelibly linked to the **ACID HOUSE** and rave scenes. Also "E," "X," or "XTC." Some have speculated that MDMA use can cause brain damage, whereas others suggest it's the other way round.

edge city *noun* A conurbation that began as one of the su**BURBS** of a larger city but, with time, has developed its own business and entertainment center or downtown. Used as a place-name by Alex Cox in his 1984 cult classic "Repo Man" for the soulless, bland, bleached out, endless Californian suburban landscape in which it is set. "Edge City" was also an alternative title of Cox's 1978–80 UCLA student movie, which takes place in a region he later described as "a vile, horribly polluted megalopolis, [... an] asylum on the edge of Nothing, 'Where the Debris Meets the Sea.'"[1] *"Assessed by the same standards, the Virginia edge city of Tysons is bigger than downtown Miami." (From "Landscape Architecture" journal, 1988.)*

edged *adjective* Angry, annoyed, put on edge. **VALSPEAK**.

elite *adjective* In the very early days of civilian computer networking bulletin board systems (BBSes) enabled users to engage in discus-

---

1. A reference to Venice Beach, Venice, Los Angeles. Specifically, to the Venice Pavilion amphitheater, legendary 1980s–'90s skate and graffiti spot also known as the "Venice Pit." Now mostly demolished, parts of the Pavilion remain as the Venice Public Art Walls.

sion, share (usually pirated) files, and generally annoy one another. Users with elevated permissions were referred to as "elite," from which derived "leet" and various character-substituting **HACKER** ("h4x0r") language equivalents such as "3l1t3," "leet," "l33t," "1337," and so on (this type of word modification later became known as "leetspeak"). The term soon became applicable to skillful hackers in general, often applied sarcastically.

Eurofag *noun* An effeminate European male. Or any European person whatsoever. Often applied to the invasive species of androgynous British **NEW WAVE** acts such as Duran Duran, which seems pretty unreasonable considering that America has to answer for, among others, Mötley Crüe.[1] See also **FAG, ARTFAG**. *"I've gotten everyone to sign this petition, even the ones who think Big Fun are tuneless Eurofags." (From "Heathers," 1989.)*

Eurotrash *noun* Derogatory term for tacky, vapid European nouveau riche types infesting nightclubs, resorts, country clubs, etc. *"Hey babe, I negotiate million dollar deals for breakfast. I think I can handle this Eurotrash." (From "Die Hard," 1988.)*

even *interjection* See **NOT EVEN**.

ew *interjection* **VAL**acious expression of disgust, usually feigned. See **ZOD** for usage example.

excellent *adjective* Conveys the standard English meaning, but often used in surprising and inventive new ways or simply as a colloquial interjection: impressive, amazing, tremendous. *"Be excellent to each other!" (From "Bill & Ted's Excellent Adventure," 1989.)*

eye candy *noun* Something sweet to look at. Either an attractive person or, in the creative industries, striking visual imagery. In both senses there is the connotation that the subject is unlikely to pose an intellectual challenge. See also **EAR CANDY, BRAIN CANDY**. *"Decorously arranged about the 'set,' the products themselves come on like a bevy of Michele Marshes and Chuck Scarboroughs[2] – eye candy with authority." (From "Yuppie Porn" by Bruce Handy, Spy Magazine, December 1987.)*

---

1. The Crüe's epicene lead singer, Vince Neil, was reportedly the inspiration for Aerosmith's 1987 hit "Dude (Looks Like a Lady)." In "Walk This Way: The Autobiography of Aerosmith," Steven Tyler is quoted as saying, "One day we met Mötley Crüe, and they're all going, '**DUDE**!' Dude this and Dude that, everything was Dude. 'Dude (Looks Like a Lady)' came out of that session."
2. TV news anchors of the era.

face! *interjection* Exclamation interchangeable with **BURN!** indicating that the recipient has conclusively and humiliatingly lost an argument. Abbreviation of "In your face!" Also, as a verb, to humiliate someone ("Joey faced Bob by calling him a dicklizard").

face plant *noun* A particularly inelegant face-first fall in skiing, skateboarding, or any other sport or activity, which apparently or actually leaves one in an inverted position with one's head planted in the snow, earth, etc. Also "face-plant" and (especially as verb) "face-plant." *"Rate-a-Fall is a great game. [...] Spotting the highest-scoring fall on the lift wins a beer. [...] 9 [points]: Face plant with blood loss; beginning skiers flying into liftline." (From "Ski" magazine, March 1983.)*

fade *noun* A haircut of military origin in which the length of hair graduates from a shaved area (usually the back and sides of the head) to the full desired length in the space of a few inches. Very popular in the mid- to late 1980s, the hi-top fade – in which the fade develops into an elevated flattop – is exemplified by Christopher "Kid" Reid from the **HIP HOP** duo Kid 'n Play and was also a trademark of carnivorous singer Grace Jones. *"The relatively conservative 'fade' haircut is a hit with recording artists [...] as well as college and professional basketball players." (From "Ebony" magazine, September 1989.)*

fag *noun* In traditional slang, a gay male (derogatory). The term's usage in 1980s teen slang was somewhat different, referring instead to a person perceived to be weak, annoying, pretentious, or otherwise contemptible, often without explicit reference to sexuality. The insult was still concurrently used in its more conventional sense, though generally by an older demographic. *"Whoa! – Ted, you're alive!" "Yeah! I fell out of my suit when I hit the floor." "Fag!" (From "Bill & Ted's Excellent Adventure," 1989.)*

fag bag *noun* Derisive term for the "fanny pack" (US) or "bum bag" (UK). In fact, the invention of a disparaging term for this hideous item was entirely superfluous, as the two countries' names for the bag would be equally insulting when switched US/UK; "bum" (UK: "posterior") meaning a vagrant in the US, and "fanny" (US: "posterior") referring to the female genitalia in UK usage. *"This purse is commonly referred to as a 'fag-bag,' and the most noted users of this type of 'holster are the embassy folks and the SFers [Special Forces]." (From "Gung-ho: The Magazine for the International Military Man," 1984.)*

fag tag *noun* The small loop of fabric between the shoulders of a button-down shirt, correctly known as a "locker loop" and designed so the shirt can be hung from a locker-room hook and thus avoid wrinkling. Those who disdained the **PREPPY** or **NERD**y nature of the typical wearer (hence the disparaging term) would, given the opportunity, often attempt to use the "tag" for its intended purpose but without first removing the shirt's occupant.

fantabulous *adjective* Tremendously good – a portmanteau word blending "fantastic" and "fabulous." *"Texas Instruments has got a little portable terminal. [...] Anyplace you've got an electric plug and a telephone, you're on line. And what you're on line to is the most fantabulous thing you ever could have imagined in your wildest dreams." (From the remarks of Nicholas Johnson, "Information for the 1980's [sic]: Final Report of the White House Conference on Library and Information Services, 1979," January 1, 1980.)*

fatty *noun* A particularly bulbous marijuana cigarette.

fave *noun* Truncation of "favorite." Often used by females to enthusiastically describe their media heartthrobs and associated music, movies, etc. *"Oh, I just love polo. It's one of my real fave raves." (From the "Miami Vice" episode "Little Prince," 1984.)*

faze *verb* To fluster, annoy, or unnerve someone. The word dates back at least to the 1800s but was in unusually popular usage in the 1980s. *"I mean, the man's got ice in his veins." "Oh dear, that does sound serious." "It's an expression, KITT. It means nothing fazed him. It's like he doesn't care about anything." (From the "Knight Rider" episode "Brother's Keeper," 1983.)*

fenced *adjective* See **EDGED**.

fer sher *interjection* See **FOR SURE**.

fine *adjective* Of a person, attractive, hot. Not merely sexy but actually quite awe-inspiring. *(Ref. "Somebody's Baby" by Jackson Browne, from the soundtrack of "Fast Times at Ridgemont High," 1982.)*

fist sandwich *noun* A punch in the mouth; pithier variant of the older "knuckle sandwich." *"And if anybody yells at you, they get a fist sandwich from me." (From "Who Framed Mary Bubnik?" – "Bad News Ballet" series #4 – by Jahnna N. Malcolm, 1989)*

five-o *noun* The police or any member(s) thereof. Originates from the 1968–80 TV cop show "Hawaii Five-O" which chose the moniker simply because Hawaii was the fiftieth US state to join the Union. Some claim the term came from the "5.0" badge on the fenders of the (Fox-body) Ford Mustang SSP (Special Service Package) produced between 1982 and 1990 and popular with law enforcement agencies such as the California Highway Patrol, but this is likely either a coincidence or a deliberate in-joke by Ford. *"Damn! Five-O! [...] Bailin' out, Jack!" (From the "Miami Vice" episode "Made for Each Other," 1985.)*

flake *noun* An unreliable person or one who is apparently incapable of getting a grip on life and making something of himself or herself. Thus, "flaky" (adjective): unreliable, "flake out" (verb): to let someone down, usually by failing to show up or otherwise pull one's weight, having promised to do so. The term is recorded in this usage as far back as the early 1960s, found particularly in baseball, and is perhaps related to earlier drug subculture use, "flake" having been a term for cocaine back to the 1920s. Also, by the 1980s hippies were universally well-known for being both entirely unreliable and also flaky in the physical sense, due to poor bodily hygiene leading to "dermatitis neglecta," so there is at least a connotative connection there (see also **CRUNCHY**). *"Delia, you are a flake. You have always been a flake. If you insist on frightening people, do it with your sculpture." (From "Beetlejuice," 1988.)*

flame *verb* Early **HACKER** slang, appearing in "The Jargon File" (a glossary of computer programmers' guild language, also known as "The Hacker's Dictionary") as early as 1983, defined therein somewhat differently to the more modern Internet usage (to attack or insult someone). Originally, this meant simply to engage in heated discussion, ranting, sounding off, etc., particularly at tedious length and/or in utterly pointless fashion, on a topic unworthy of such attention.

flamer *noun* A flamboyantly camp gay male; this usage dates back at least to the 1940s. Also one who engages in flaming (see **FLAME**).

flash *adjective* Cool, exciting, showy, slick. Possibly encouraged by Dino De Laurentiis' extremely camp space opera "Flash Gordon," and its equally flamboyant theme song by Queen. *(Ref. "Flash's Theme" by Queen, from the soundtrack of the movie "Flash Gordon," 1980.)*

flavor *noun* Unique personal style as expressed in behavior, clothing, art, or some other manner, exhibiting savoir faire, skill, and panache. Also "flava." *(Ref. "Express Yourself" by NWA, 1988).*

floppy *noun* Floppy disk: an antiquated computer storage medium, common from the 1970s until the early 2000s. In use by the US military up until 2019 for relatively unimportant, non-mission-critical systems such as the Strategic Automated Command and Control System (SACCS), which manages the nation's land-launched nuclear missiles, long-range strategic nuclear attack aircraft, and nuclear-armed strike submarines. Floppy disks typically came in the original 8-inch and later 5¼-inch sizes, both of which were actually flexible. In contrast, the subsequent 3½-inch variety was encased in a hard plastic shell, with a sliding metal gate that protected the data storage medium from fingerprints and other catastrophes. If you've ever wondered why the ubiquitous "save" icon is inexplicably unintuitive, it's because the icon is a representation of a 3½-inch floppy. *"Floppy disks are pretty expensive." (From "Sixteen Candles," 1984.)*

Fig. 6: Floppy Disk Comparison

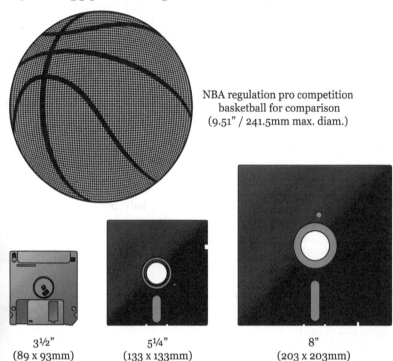

NBA regulation pro competition
basketball for comparison
(9.51" / 241.5mm max. diam.)

3½"	5¼"	8"
(89 x 93mm)	(133 x 133mm)	(203 x 203mm)

fly *adjective* Hip, cool, fashionable. Originating in the 1930s, the term enjoyed a resurgence following the slew of '70s Blaxploitation movies; this popularity continued into '80s **HIP HOP** culture. *(Ref. "The New Style," by Beastie Boys, 1986.)*

fool *noun* A naive, unaware person. One who can easily be taken advantage of, or who is operating under an immense delusion and is thus likely to **GET SCHOOLED**. Depending on manner of use, the term can be intended either as a serious insult, mild rebuke, or friendly sobriquet. Contrary to popular belief, Mr. T's use of the phrase "I pity the fool" originated in the movie "Rocky III" (see citation) and was never employed by the character BA Baracus in "The A-Team"; though he often referred to HM Murdock as a "fool" and many others as "suckas" (see **SUCKER**). The popular phrase also featured in a reference to Mr. T's tireless and exceptionally wide-ranging merchandising efforts in 1985's "Pee-Wee's Big Adventure" ("I pity the poor fool who don't eat my cereal"). *"No, I don't hate Balboa, but I pity the fool." (From "Rocky III," 1982.)*

for cear *interjection* **"for sir"** Seriously, really. Abbreviation of "for certain," employed in both inquisitive and emphatic uses. See also **FOR SURE**.

FOR SURE

for sure *interjection* **"fer sherr"** Definitely, affirmative, you bet! Another key component of the **VALLEY GIRL**'s linguistic arsenal, to the extent that it was included in the title of the book "Fer Shurr! How To Be A Valley Girl – Totally!"[1] Also used as an exclamation to add emphasis to the preceding statement: "I'm going to the Galleria. For sure!" or, when employed in a particularly drawn-out fashion, sarcastically: "Like I'd ever go out with him! As if! Ferr Sherrrrr!" *(Ref. "Valley Girl" by Frank Zappa, 1982.)*

four-one-one, 411 *noun* Information: the lowdown, the gen, the dirt, the inside scoop. Derives from the phone number for directory assistance.

fox *noun* An attractive person. In 1980s usage usually a female but also applicable to a male. *"She's a fox, man. A fox. She could go with any guy on campus, and she probably will if I don't show up." (From "Vonnie and Monique" – "Keepsake" series #7 – by Dorothy Francis, 1987.)*

freak *noun* An attractive, uninhibited young lady. See also **FREAK OUT** (verb). *(Ref. "Super Freak" by Rick James, 1981.)*

freaking *adjective* Minced oath: euphemism for "fucking" and employed in an identically intensifying way. Used in this way as far back as the late 1920s. *"It's only booby traps. Why you being such a sissy?" "Freakin' kids!" (From "The Goonies," 1985.)*

freak out *verb* To completely lose emotional control due to extreme excitement, happiness, anger, fear, etc. Also simply "freak." *"My mother would freak out if she knew I was going up there with you." (From "Back to the Future," 1985.)*

freebase *noun* See **BASE**.

freeware *noun* Computer software legally available without charge, usually produced by small companies or hobbyists. See also **SHAREWARE**. Precursor to open-source software, but with the major difference that the source code of freeware is (generally) neither made publicly visible nor released from copyright. Many freeware programs were comparatively small applications, intended as utilities to solve small or niche use cases, or as a basic beta version of more complex programs to be released commercially in the future. *"Each improving version is a legacy to the generous, talented people who make Freeware – and the hobby in general – work." (From "InfoWorld" magazine September 1982.)*

fresh *adjective* **HIP HOP** term: **COOL**, new, funky, crisp, sharp. *(Ref. "Rock the House," by DJ Jazzy Jeff & the Fresh Prince, 1987.)*

fresh one *noun* A punch in the face. The implication is that the previously-supplied injury (and the lesson it was intended to emphasize to the recipient) is starting to fade and may require renewed application: "I'll give you a fresh one."

frick *verb* A minced oath; euphemism for "fuck." "Frick and Frack" was also a (rare, as implied by the citation) reference to the testicles

---

1. By Mary Corey and Victoria Westermark, 1982.

originating rather obscurely from a pair of 1930s Swiss trick skaters. *"And then we gonna deprive you of your ... Frick and Frack." "I don't understand a word of it, do you?" (From "Action Jackson," 1988.)*

frigging *adjective* See **FREAKING**.

frost *verb* To make angry, infuriate. Often in reference to a body part ("That really frosts my balls").

frosty *adjective* Exceptionally cool and, by implication, ready for anything. *"We're all in strung out shape. But stay frosty and alert." (From "Aliens," 1986.)*

fucking a *interjection* **"fucking eh"** Not strictly a 1980s term, having been around for many years previously, but in very common use during the decade. Generally, an expression of emphatic agreement or affirmation akin to "You're damn right!" Some have suggested an etymology based on "A-1" or "A-number-one" but it is more likely to have derived from military use of the term "affirmative" in acknowledgment of an order or statement. "Affirmative" becomes, under duress of arduous or tense conditions, "fucking affirmative," which under further stress becomes the even less formal "fuckin' A." In some circles the term is used sarcastically as an expression of annoyance or disappointment synonymous with "dammit!" *"They're from Stars and Stripes, they'll make you famous." "Fucking A! Yeah!" (From "Full Metal Jacket," 1987.)*

fucknut *noun* An incompetent, irritating idiot; perhaps eccentric and possibly crazy, but mainly stupid in a manner dangerous to those around him. It is tempting to suggest the derivation jokingly implied in the citation (from "screw" to "fuck" and "ball" to "nut"), but the term is more likely to be an abbreviation of "fucking nutcase" or, more simply, one whose "nut" (see **NUTBAR**) is "fucked" – i.e., malfunctioning. *"Base humour, too, which pits Sonny's screwball (fucknut?) mentality against the strict social mores of Capitol." (From "The Time Out Film Guide" by Tom Milne, 1989.)*

fuck them if they can't take a joke *phrase* Sardonic expression of military origin indicating a lack of sympathy with the victim(s) of some mishap. Equivalent to **SHIT HAPPENS**. *"What're we gonna tell the cops? 'Fuck it if she can't take a joke, Sarge'?" (From "Heathers," 1989.)*

fuck you, Watson *phrase* An admirably simple retort to the **NO SHIT, SHERLOCK** zinger.

fugly *adjective* "Fucking ugly." A popular euphemism in the 2000s but dating back to the early '80s. Regular ugliness may be described as an absence of beauty tending toward disharmony, but something that is fugly is guilty of deliberate, egregious aesthetic vandalism (e.g., **HAMMER PANTS**). Also "fuggly," as in the citation. *"Man, the ASCII-to-EBCDIC code in that printer driver is fuggly." (From "The New Hacker's Dictionary," by Eric S. Raymond, 1991.)*

funky-fresh *adjective* Exciting, new, stylish, hip. *"Are you two Run-DMC?" "Funky fresh, in the flesh." (From "Krush Groove," 1985.)*

gag me *interjection* Exclamation of disgust, deriving from the earlier "gagged" (disgusted) and possibly related to the maxim that something particularly repugnant would "gag a maggot." *"I don't want to, like, start a family. Like, God, I'd get all puffed out to the max and all, for sure!" "Oh, God, gag me. How could you?" (From "Valley Girl," 1983.)*

gag me with a spoon *interjection* The acme (or nadir, depending on perspective) of **VALSPEAK**. Elaboration on **GAG ME** intended to express extreme disgust. Due to the body image issues often experienced by such young women, the term may derive from the practice of avoiding caloric intake by using a spoon to self-induce vomiting via the pharyngeal reflex. *(Ref. "Valley Girl" by Frank Zappa, 1982.)*

gal pal *noun* A female friend, usually of a woman.

game *verb* To woo or attempt to seduce someone. The slightly older (1960s–70s) version of the verb meant to trick, con, or deceive. There is a shady connotation in this usage also; the game of love is both strategic and tactical (see also **SCAM**). Also (noun) as "got game," to have the ability to influence the opposite sex. *(Ref. "I Ain't tha 1" by NWA, 1988.)*

gang bang *verb* To engage in street gang related activities, particularly those involved with fighting rival outfits. Also to engage in group sex (see **BANG**). Context should make it clear which sense is intended, but often does not. *(Ref. "Gangsta Gangsta" by NWA, 1988.)*

gangsta *noun* A member of a street gang, involved in low-level criminal activity centered around the retail distribution of contraband narcotics. Derived but distinct from "gangster," which refers mainly to those involved in the **BOOTLEG** alcohol trade during the Prohibition era and other such established, respectable racketeers. As an adjective, alluding to aspects of the life of such individuals, particularly in the case of "gangsta **RAP**." *(Ref. "Gangsta Gangsta" by NWA, 1988.)*

gank *verb* To rob, steal from, **JACK**, or defraud someone. Also (as a noun) marijuana. For both meanings a phonesthemic word (related to "yank" in the first sense and **DANK** in the second, for example). Later in the '90s both meanings would coincide; the term came to refer to fake crack cocaine, fraudulently sold as the real thing. *(Ref. "No More ?s" by Eazy-E, 1988.)*

geek *noun* Derives from the carnival sideshow of the early 20th century, where the "geek show" would consist of a person performing outrageous, obnoxious, or transgressive acts such as biting the heads off live chickens and snakes. Consequently, by the 1980s a "geek" had come to mean a kid whose studious dedication and consequent neglect of all other aspects of life had resulted in a similarly atrophied set of social skills. See also **NERD, DORK, DWEEB, CHUD, ZOD.** *"Do I look like Mother Teresa? If I did, I probably wouldn't mind talking to the geek squad." (From "Heathers," 1989.)*

generic *adjective* Low-quality, shoddy, tedious, badly done, **BOOTLEG.** At best, undifferentiated, off-brand, or stock. *(Ref. "Gin Guzzlin' Frenzy" by Mojo Nixon & Skid Roper, 1987.)*

get a life *phrase* Retort suggesting that the target should seek broader horizons, due to being a boring, obsessive, or infantile **NERD** without the experience of the wider world necessary to develop a sense of proportion. Not to be confused with Rick James' excellent 1981 single "Ghetto Life" about escaping the destructive tedium of poverty, though the exhortative lyrical substitution of "Get a life!" in the chorus is quite fitting. *(Ref. "Get a Life" by Soul II Soul, 1990.)*

get bent *interjection* Interjection meaning "get lost," "go away."

get blitz *verb* See **BLITZ.**

get horizontal *verb* To have sex. *"All you care about is getting horizontal." (From the "Alien Nation" episode "The First Cigar," 1989.)*

get out *interjection* Expression of surprise and (often feigned) disbelief or incredulity ("Get out of here"). Usually used sincerely, but occasionally sarcastically (synonymously with **NO SHIT, SHERLOCK**). See also **TAKE OFF.** *(Ref. "Take Off" by Bob & Doug McKenzie, 1981.)*

get real *interjection* Exhortation inviting the subject to face reality and rid himself of the fanciful notions that caused him to utter whatever nonsense prompted the response. *(Ref. "How Ya Like Me Now," by Kool Moe Dee, 1987.)*

get schooled *verb* To learn a lesson the hard way. *(Ref. "I Ain't tha 1" by NWA, 1988.)*

get with it *phrase* Encouragement to get up to speed with something, understand some concept, get on board with something. *"Think things over, Callahan. Get with it. It's a whole new ball game these days." (From "Sudden Impact," 1983.)*

get with the program *phrase* Similar to **GET WITH IT,** but with the added and slightly menacing Orwellian connotation that one is refusing to accept a set of ideas that one's peer group has willingly internalized and that such a failure to comply is ... regrettable. *"Hey, John, I think you can get with the program a little, huh?" (From "Die Hard," 1988.)*

get your arms around *phrase* To understand something to a full, encompassing extent; to grok. *"It has taken this committee months to get our arms around this thing at this point. You found out it was pretty tough in a few days to get your arms around it, didn't you?" (From question by Representative Bill McCollum (R-FL), "Iran-Contra Investigation: Joint Hearings Before the House Select Committee to Investigate Covert Arms Transactions with Iran and the Senate Select Committee on Secret Military Assistance to Iran and the Nicaraguan Opposition," June 1987.)*

ghetto blaster *noun* See **BOOMBOX**. *[Scientist touches a button on boombox, firing a rocket that obliterates the target dummy.] "Something we're making for the Americans. It's called a ghetto blaster." (From "James Bond: The Living Daylights," 1987.)*

ghetto sled *noun* A large, older, domestic luxury auto such as a Cadillac, Lincoln, etc. – a land yacht – in abominable condition, often highly and poorly modified, held together with duct tape and hope. A **HOOPTIE**. Aficionados optimistically call the rust "patina."

glam *adjective* Glamorous. A holdover from the 1970s glam rock fad, imported to the US from the UK via David Bowie, which then evolved into the 1980s glam metal (or hair metal) genre of **HEAVY METAL** – think Mötley Crüe, Twisted Sister, Poison, etc. – abetted by the "second British invasion" of the US charts by **NEW ROMANTIC** themed music and visuals in the early '80s. *(Ref. "Alphabet St." by Prince, 1988.)*

glom onto *verb* To acquisitively grab something and keep hold of it in limpet-like fashion. From the Scots "glaum" – to grab or snatch. Often used in the figurative sense of understanding and internalizing an idea, to "catch onto" something (see **GET YOUR ARMS AROUND**). *"Now, if your only job were to glom onto precious stones and nuggets, then you might say there wasn't that much to dig in 'Digger.'" (From "PC" magazine, April 1984.)*

gnarly *adjective* Originally surfer slang for something particularly dangerous or difficult ("Gnarly wave!") adopted by 1980s popular culture as a synonym for "excellent" ("Gnarly hairdo!"). In many circles the term maintained both meanings simultaneously, though the negative sense tended toward "impressively disgusting," as in the citation. *"I heard it was really gnarly. She sucked down a bowl of multi-purpose deodorizing disinfectant and then SMASH!" (From "Heathers," 1989.)*

go ahead, make my day *phrase* Invitation to an adversary to make the first aggressive move, after which the speaker may act in legitimate self-defense and, by implication, clean the adversary's **CLOCK** in a satisfying, cathartic way. Also an expression of general defiance indicating that one is not bothered by a threatened action, much like the Duke of Wellington's famous "Publish and be damned." The phrase's popularity originates from its use by Clint Eastwood in the fourth Dirty Harry movie (see citation) and its subsequent use by President Ronald Reagan in 1985. *"Go ahead. Make my day." (From "Sudden Impact," 1983.)*

go for the gusto *phrase* Exhortation to approach life with vivacity, similar to "Work hard, play hard." The phrase earned its place in the public consciousness as one of several famous, long-running promotional slogans for Schlitz beer. This was before the brand was killed off, starting in the late 1970s, firstly by a series of disastrously ill-considered ads that collectively became known as the "Drink Schlitz or I'll Kill You" campaign, and secondly by a management strategy of "salami slicing" reductions in product quality that is now known in business school circles as "The Schlitz Mistake." Perhaps because of these missteps or simply its unironic, gung-ho nature the phrase was often employed sarcastically, such as when presented with a direly unsatisfactory situation from which no joy could conceivably be squeezed ("Cornflakes for dinner, again?" "Go for the gusto!") *"We need to go for the gusto! We need to enjoy our tasks, enjoy our challenges." (From "Swimming World" magazine, 1987.)*

going together *phrase* Dating; "going steady." *"Now, as you all know, Darryl and Lisa have been going together for quite some time." (From "Coming to America," 1988.)*

Gold Coast *noun* A coastal section of south Florida including Miami-Dade, Broward, and Palm Beach counties, so called because of the wealth accumulated there. Popularized by the TV show Miami Vice, whose Organized Crime Bureau was run under cover of a front operation named the Gold Coast Shipping Co. Headquartered in an eye-catching Art Moderne two-story office building (actually the premises of the Miami Shipbuilding Corporation – at the time of filming known as the Miami Shipyards Corp.) at 615 SW 2nd Avenue, the building is sadly now demolished. "Gold Coast" was also the preproduction title of the pilot script that would become "Miami Vice." *"Gold Coast resorts such as Miami Beach, Fort Lauderdale (which gained notoriety as a sandbox for the college set) and Palm Beach (a favorite winter retreat for wealthy socialites) are synonymous with vacation glamor." (From "The Old South" by John Osborne, 1988.)*

goober *noun* A harmless dolt. An insult, but usually a reasonably friendly one.

goon *noun* A slang term dating back to 1919 or earlier. Originally a stupid person. In evolved use in the '70s and '80s to refer to a cop, paid thug, or other hired muscle (though still implying suboptimal intelligence). *(Ref. "Fashion" by David Bowie, 1983.)*

goth *noun* A nonconformist individual, easily identifiable as such due to his or her strict conformity to a dress code of black jeans, large boots and leather jacket or coat (bad weather permitting). Another British cultural import to the US, "modern" gothism is generally seen as a more intellectually focused offshoot of 1970s punk, but the subculture traces its roots back to the gothic literature of the 18th and 19th centuries (Shelley, Coleridge, Byron, Poe, etc.) and an interest in various (quasi-)religious or philosophical pursuits of yesteryear. Perhaps due to this deep historical foundation, gothicists persist today (at the time of writing), the '80s subculture having spawned numerous offshoots in the '90s and since. Goths of all types were united by their vitriolic resistance to the suggestion that they were in fact goths, and in some extreme cases found it difficult to even speak or write the word (as in the citation). *"I'm not interested in what g***s think." (Andrew Eldritch, lead singer of The Sisters of Mercy, seminal '80s goth band.)*

gotta motor *phrase* See **MOTOR**.

granola-eater *noun* A hippie, particularly one with greater than average concerns about the environment. *"My son could become a treehugging granola-eater." (From "Surfer" magazine, 1988.)*

greenmail *noun*   The act of purchasing a large quantity of a company's shares and threatening a hostile takeover, but then offering the shares back to the company at an inflated price. Portmanteau of "greenback" and "blackmail" – although the hustle is similar to extortion, not blackmail, as there is no threat of releasing damaging information. A favorite tactic of the corporate raider. See also **POISON PILL**. *"You're here on a hostile takeover and you grab us for some greenmail." (From "Die Hard," 1988.)*

greenwash *verb*   Of a company, government, or other group, to fashionably pay lip service to environmentally friendly concerns, usually while doing little or nothing to change destructive practices, in the context of a rise in "green" sensibilities during the 1980s. *"They fear that Conable's green rhetoric is little more than a 'greenwash.'" (From "New Scientist" magazine, October 7, 1989.)*

grill *noun*   The teeth. Inspired by an automobile's front grille, possibly those of 1980s **BEEMER**s in particular, which looked like they had an enormous pair of Bugs-Bunny-type buck teeth. *(Ref. "Personal" by Ice-T, 1988.)*

grimbo *noun*   An unattractive, physically unpleasant, and generally uninteresting person: one who is grim. Rhyming antonym of **BIMBO**. *"The strongest competition to 'squid' and 'grimbo' as successor term to 'nerd' is 'dexter.'" (From "New York Times" magazine's "On Language" column, by William Safire, September 22, 1985.)*

grindage *noun*   Food. Example of the **-AGE** suffix applied to "grind" (as in to chew; to grind between the teeth). Thus, that which may be chewed. California origin. Note: while use of this term is believably claimed in subcultural use beginning in the (later) 1980s, the earliest available instance in pop culture is from 1992's "Encino Man" (released as "California Man" in Europe) – see citation – which popularized the term in the mainstream. *"Mr. Morgan, if you're edged 'cuz I'm wheezin' on your grindage, just chill. If I had the whole Brady Bunch thing happenin' at my pad, I'd go grind over there." (From "Encino Man," 1992.)*

grit *noun*   A dirty or apparently dirty individual; specifically one whose appearance is influenced by his interests in automobile customization and **HEAVY METAL** music, resulting in him and his jeans, band T-shirt and bandana being begrimed with various substances. See also **HESSIAN**. *"[Teens] even use a vocabulary which is not meant to be understood by anyone outside of the group. Some 'tribal membership' teen lingo which was overheard recently included: [...] grits, hosers, slime and scuzz." (From TEAM, the Early Adolescence Magazine, Volume 1, 1986.)*

grody *adjective*   Disgusting, distasteful, **GROSS**. Originally (1960s) "groty" (related to the synonymous UK slang "grotty"), indicating the word's derivation as an abbreviation of "grotesque." Also the Polish word for "castles" – so technically it's not impolite to say that Polish castles are grody. *"Like, you know, I hear there's something really grody about the air in Hollywood, you know?" (From "Valley Girl," 1983.)*

grody to the max *phrase* Unbelievably **GRODY**. Too grody for words. Grodissimo. See also **TO THE MAX**. *(Ref. "Valley Girl" by Frank Zappa, 1982.)*

gross *adjective* Disgusting, hideous, grievously macabre. *"Aren't you scared?" "I'm not scared of sheets. Are you gross under there? Are you Night of the Living Dead under there?" (From "Beetlejuice," 1988.)*

gross me out *phrase* To shock someone into a state of revulsion. *"Would you feel better if you knew one of my secrets?" "Don't gross me out." (From "Sixteen Candles," 1984.)*

gross me out the door *phrase* To shock someone into a state of such extreme revulsion that they have to leave the room. **VALSPEAK**.

guac *noun* Abbreviation of "guacamole," ubiquitous feature of California's culinary landscape. *"My English friends insisted on putting a handful of crisps (potato chips) on their plates, spooning the guac over them and eating the mess with a knife and fork." (From "Some Like it Hotter" by Geraldine Duncann, 1985.)*

hack *noun* In early computer user jargon, a hack was a solution to a problem that worked, but in a nonstandard ("non-canonical") and probably inefficient, jury-rigged manner. The term later overcame its negative connotations to mean a clever, original solution to an intractable problem and (verb) in more general terms, to work on something (with the assumption that the work required intensive, creative problem solving). *"The word 'hack' doesn't really have sixty-nine different meanings. [...] In fact, [it has only] one, which defies articulation." (From "The Hacker's Dictionary," 1983 edition.)*

hacker *noun* One who **HACK**s. An intelligent computer user who is interested in how hardware/software works rather than just how to use it. A technical expert in any field. Also, in a negative sense, "a malicious or inquisitive meddler who tries to discover information by poking around."[1] The term gained mainstream popularity when Hollywood realized, post "WarGames" (1983), that they could semi-plausibly explain away any computer-related deus ex machina baloney by simply invoking "hackers." *"You're thinking, 'That female chick is some sort of super-hacker or something.'" (From "Short Circuit," 1986.)*

hairball *noun* A repulsive person, particularly a small-time street criminal. Derives from the thick, unpleasant clumps of matted hair commonly **BARF**ed up by cats and other self-grooming furry animals. *"Come on, hairball! Cut down on that shit, man!" (From "Major League," 1989.)*

hair metal *noun* See **GLAM**.

hairy *adjective* Of a situation, dangerous, touch-and-go. Also indicative of monstrosity, as in "big, hairy deal." *"If any of that stuff goes up in smoke, we're gonna be in for a hairy time around here." (From "Superman III," 1983.)*

Hammer pants *noun* Astonishing broccoli-legged clothing based on the harem pant and popularized by MC Hammer in the late 1980s and early '90s. Tapered at the ankle, fairly tight around the calf, extremely baggy everywhere else, with a very saggy rise creating a significant volume of material and, visually, a bizarre false crotchline around the knee. Suitable for energetic dancing, the billows of rippling material often inducing an unsettling mesmeric effect in the observer. Often conflated with **PARACHUTE PANTS**, possibly because many examples were constructed from parachute-type silk or similar man-made materials, or (also) that the square yardage of material required and/or the volume of air captured within might itself be suf-

---

1. From "The Hacker's Dictionary," 1983; see **FLAME**.

ficient for use as a parachute. See Fig. 9 on page 86 for an illustration of the difference.

hang *verb* To hang out, spend time with, **CHILL**.

happening *adjective* Hip, chic, current, trendy. A hangover from the recent, deeply unfashionable 1970s and thus often used quite sarcastically.

happy camper *noun* One who is relaxed and at ease. Originates in the world of summer camps, whose operators encourage the inmates to be contented, despite being away from home and surrounded by venomous fauna. Usually used in the negative ("not a happy camper") to describe someone exhibiting undesirable emotions ranging from mild displeasure to explosive rage. *"You know he'll show. Be a happy camper." (From "Thrashin'," 1986.)*

hardballer *noun* A gung-ho, no-nonsense, goal-oriented individual whose behavior borders on the thuggish. One who plays hardball. *"He was a real hardballer and made sure Rockefeller felt the cold." (From "Vice Presidential Power" by Paul Charles Light, 1984.)*

hardbody *noun* A fit, athletic, attractive woman. Also an affectionate nickname for the Nissan D21 compact truck (available in the US market from 1986) due to its tough, double-walled truckbed and simple, rugged good looks. *"'Hardbodies' are the 'perfect little foxes down at the beach.'" (From "Films and Filming" magazine, 1984.)*

hardcore *adjective* Extreme in general, also (when applied to behavior or lifestyle) focused, obsessive, uncompromising, ruthless. Also (noun) a 1980s evolution of '70s **PUNK**; largely a West Coast reaction to supposedly weak New York post-punk **NEW WAVE** acts. *"The difference between punk and hardcore is that hardcore is more sophisticated, in a way. [...] It's played a little more adventurously. The vocal style is always angry. I like that." (Dee Dee Ramone, quoted in "Punk" article, "Spin" magazine, January 1986.)*

harsh *adjective* Strict, severe, unfair, rude. *"Ooh, that's harsh. You don't bounce back from that right away." (From "When Harry Met Sally," 1989.)*

hassle *noun* A pain in the butt or annoyance, caused by deliberate hostile interference (see **BUST ONE'S BALLS**) or laborious bureaucratic BS. *"We could start the movie company again. Promote the stuff we need from the film commission." "Aw, that's always such a big hassle." (From "The A-Team" episode "Mexican Slayride," 1983.)*

have a cow *phrase* See **DON'T HAVE A COW**.

headbanger *noun* An aficionado of any of the various genres of **HEAVY METAL** music; a rocker. The term, of late '70s origin, was universalized by MTV's groundbreaking metal show "Headbanger's Ball" (1987–95) featuring both mainstream and alternative flavors. See also **HESSIAN**.

heavy *adjective* Extremely serious, extreme, or **INTENSE**. *"Remember? your mother is at that exact same dance with you!" "Right. This could get heavy, Doc." (From "Back to the Future Part 2," 1989.)*

heavy metal *noun* Stripped-down, sped-up, balls-to-the-wall[1] descendant of rock 'n roll. Emergent in the late 1960s and popular in the '70s, '80s metal developed a harder, sharper edge. Both the pop-friendly **GLAM** metal (exemplified by Mötley Crüe) and pop-hostile **THRASH** metal (exemplified by Metallica) variants enjoyed significant success. See also **HEADBANGER, HESSIAN, GRIT, SHRED, BRUTAL.** *"Why don't you take Allison to one of your heavy metal vomit parties?" (From "The Breakfast Club," 1985.)*

hecka *adverb* Extremely, superlatively. Minced version of **HELLA.**

heinous *adjective* Impressively, **AWESOME**ly bad. *"We're in danger of flunking most heinously tomorrow, Ted." (From "Bill & Ted's Excellent Adventure," 1989.)*

helicopter parent *noun* A micromanaging father or mother whose inability to leave his or her child alone for any significant period is detrimental to the development of self-reliance. *"Do not be a 'helicopter' parent. They hover over the child." (From "The Creative Child and Adult Quarterly" journal, 1987.)*

hella *adverb* "Extremely," or "a lot of." An abbreviation of "helluva," but grammatically distinct; whereas one would say, "He makes a helluva lot of money," one would say, "He makes hella money." Originally an Oakland-specific piece of slang, later spreading to the vocabulary of northern California in general. Sometimes (adjective) meaning "extremely good." See also **HECKA.** *(Ref. "On Fire" by Tone Loc, 1989.)*

hellacious *adjective* Originally extremely negative (from "hell" plus the "-acious" ending indicating possession of a quality; see also **BODACIOUS**). Very bad, difficult, evil, etc. Later flipped to an extremely positive sense: very skillful, effective, high-quality, etc. While both meanings were in use simultaneously, context would indicate intention. *"In any case, Hogue said you were, quote, 'one hellaciously fine physician.'" (From "Doc Hollywood," 1991.)*

hello, McFly? *interjection* Inquiry intended to enliven someone who is apparently asleep, stupid, not paying attention, or otherwise remarkably slow on the uptake. Originates (in a longer form) from the movie "Back to the Future" in which on multiple occasions Biff Tannen yells variations on this theme while rapping his knuckles on George McFly's cranium to discover whether anyone is available within. *"Hello! Hello, anybody home? Hey! Think McFly, think!" (From "Back to the Future," 1985.)*

herb *noun* Marijuana. Also, as a name, an insult insinuating unfashionable nerdiness. Originates from the poorly-received 1985–86 Burger King ad campaign featuring "Herb" – the only person in

---

1. Not a reference to the **NADS** as is commonly assumed, but aviation jargon. An aircraft's throttle lever (or levers, for multi-engine airplanes) would traditionally be topped with a colored ball for easy identification and gripping; to push the lever all the way forward puts it up against or near the cockpit firewall. This is what Goose should've said instead of **BALLISTIC.**

America never to have eaten at a Burger King. *(Ref. "Don't Believe the Hype" by Public Enemy, 1988.)*

hessian *noun* A serious metalhead or **HEADBANGER**. Identifiable by the mullet, band T-shirt (likely ripped or at least sleeveless), fingerless leather gloves, partially primer-painted Camaro, etc. Later morphed into "hesher." Derives from the Hessian warriors; feared German fighters who fought for the British in the War of Independence, but who were defeated by George Washington while they were hungover in Trenton, PA (according to legend).

hide the salami *phrase* Playful euphemism for sexual intercourse. *"Wait up girls, I've got a salami I've got to hide." (From "Caddyshack," 1980.)*

high five *noun* The act of slapping another person's open palm, at head-height or above, in salute and/or celebration. Though likely invented in the 1970s, the high five became the fashionable greeting of choice in the '80s. The high five's first documented occurrence was, depending on whom one believes, either between Glenn Burke and Dusty Baker of the LA Dodgers on October 2nd, 1977 or between Derek Smith and Wiley Brown of the Louisville Cardinals at some point in the 1978–79 season. *"Ain't it the truth." "Oh, it's the truth." "High-five!" "All right!" (From "Pretty in Pink," 1986.)*

high-maintenance *adjective* Of a romantic partner or other person, to require an unusually large investment of time, attention, and/or funds. Also applicable to any similarly energy-intensive object or activity, such as boat ownership. *"You're high-maintenance, but you think you're low-maintenance." (From "When Harry Met Sally," 1989.)*

himbo *noun* A male **BIMBO**; see also **BOY TOY**.

hip *adjective* **COOL**, stylish, fashionable, in-the-know. One of the few slang terms to remain more or less in vogue over the course of many decades. First reported (with this meaning) in the early 1900s, the term grew in usage with the rise of jazz in the early 20th century and thereafter with the emerging counterculture of the 1950s and '60s. In the '80s the term might have been used with a degree of sarcasm, due to it itself being moderately old-fashioned. Etymologically, "hip" in this usage has nothing to do with the original anatomical sense (despite an early claimed association with opium smokers lying on one hip while consuming the drug) but is likely to originate, via "hep," from a cry exhorting horses or other animals to get moving ("hup," "hyup," etc.) *(Ref. "Hip to Be Square" by Huey Lewis and the News, 1986.)*

hip hop *noun* Cultural phenomenon originating in the Bronx, NY, in the mid-1970s involving music performance (see **RAP**), dancing (see **BREAKDANCE**, **POPPING AND LOCKING**), DJing (see **SCRATCH**, **BEATBOX**) and graffiti (see **BOMB**, **TAG**, **RACK UP**). *"'This is all for hip hop,' he says, extending his arms in a gesture that fills the room. 'Everything I do is hip hop. I'm hip hop.'" (Derek Showard, AKA Grand Mixer D.St, AKA Grand Mixer DXT, quoted in "D.St." article, "Spin" magazine, November 1985.)*

hodad *noun* Originally surfer slang for, variously, a non-surfer who nonetheless enjoys the subculture, a wannabe surfer (pejorative), or a rowdy type of juvenile delinquent surfer. By the time the term was adopted by the surfer-admiring but largely non-surfing **VALSPEAK** subculture the pejorative sense was, ironically, prevalent. *"Crowds of Surfers that acted like Greasers also appeared in the high school, and they were called Hodad Surfers. (The metaphor, Hodad, was derived from the Surfer peer greeting: 'Ho! Dad!')" (From "Adolescent Subcultures and Delinquency" by Schwendinger and Schwendinger, 1985.)*

ho-ho *noun* A person prone to weight gain. Derives from the miniature Swiss roll cakes manufactured by Hostess. **VALSPEAK**.

Hollywood stop *noun* A driving maneuver, usually illegal, in which one does not come to a complete stop at a traffic light or stop sign but instead rolls through at walking speed. Also "California stop," "rolling stop." *"Mr. Williams also contended that the Southern Pacific Company truck driver made a 'Hollywood' stop." (From "Jury Verdicts Weekly," 1982.)*

homeboy *noun* A male friend or acquaintance from one's place of origin (hometown, neighborhood, etc.) The term later to came to imply involvement in gang activities. Also a catchall generic epithet for a friend (like "buddy," "pal," etc.) Originated in the early 1900s as a contraction of "hometown boy" in the context of young men from impoverished country districts moving to the city to find work. *"Hey, homeboy, why don't you go close that door?" (From "The Breakfast Club," 1985.)*

homefry *noun* One's close or best friend. A linguistic leap from **HOMEBOY**/**HOMEGIRL** originating from the popular breakfast dish of skillet-fried potato chunks.

homegirl *noun* Female equivalent of **HOMEBOY**. *"Hey, homegirl, what's happening?" (From "Wildcats," 1986.)*

homey *noun* Shortened form of **HOMEBOY**. Also "homie." *"He ain't home? Aww, homey ain't home." (From "I'm Gonna Git You Sucka," 1988.)*

hood *noun* Clipping of "neighborhood," particularly in reference to inner city life. Also a criminal ("hoodlum"). *(Ref. "Boyz-n-the-Hood" by Eazy-E, 1987.)*

hook up *verb* To meet up with someone, often but by no means exclusively implying the expectation of sex. Also to make an electrical or mechanical connection between machines. *"Jim follows Susan all over the country. [...] They send messages back and forth, that's how they hook up. (From "Desperately Seeking Susan," 1985.)*

hoops *noun* Basketball. *(Ref. "Boyz-n-the-Hood" by Eazy-E, 1987.)*

hooptie *noun* An old, beat-up, unreliable, but once-luxurious and desirable automobile; usually a large, domestic marque. See also **GHETTO SLED**. The term derives from "Coupe de," as in "Coupe de Ville," Cadillac's prestige trim level from the late 1940s and later a model in its own right. *(Ref. "My Hooptie" by Sir Mix-a-Lot, 1989.)*

hoo-ride *noun* See **HOOPTIE**.

hork *verb* To steal (Canadian). Also to **BARF**. *"Jeez, who'd want to hork our clothes, eh?" (From "The Adventures of Bob & Doug McKenzie: Strange Brew," 1983.)*

horndog *noun* One for whom sex is a primary focus. A play on the culinary term "corndog."

hose monster *noun* A nymphomaniac or, in more modern terms, a female sufferer from hypersexuality. *"Who knows what kind of thrill-seeking hose monster he's got stashed in there." (From "Dragnet," 1987.)*

hoser *noun* A Canadian dingus, doofus, dolt, oaf, simpleton, yokel, or clodhopper. Also "hose-head." Popularized by Bob and Doug McKenzie (Rick Moranis and Dave Thomas) in their "The Great White North" sketches. "Hosed" is Canadian slang for "drunk"; "hoosier" was also loggers' slang for an unskilled or clumsy worker. The term was used far less by Canadians than by people imitating Canadians for comedic effect. *"Take off, you hoser!" "You take off, you knob." (From "The Adventures of Bob & Doug McKenzie: Strange Brew," 1983.)*

hotbox *verb* The act of smoking marijuana in a small, unventilated place such as a vehicle, for maximum effect and/or reasons of economy. Also (noun) an illegal cable receiver.

hotdogger *noun* An experienced surfer.

hot shit *noun* Special, remarkably good. A person or thing who is **SHIT-HOT**. *"Point number two is ya' gotta think you're hot shit. Deep down, ya' gotta think ya' got somethin' comin' to ya' because you're such hot shit." (From "The Greatest Slump of All Time" by David Carkeet, 1984.)*

house *noun* A form of up-tempo dance music, typically employing drum machine rhythms, repeated samples (often vocals), synth and/or electric piano riffs. All such elements were comparatively easily replicated on inexpensive consumer-level hardware, leading to an energetic grassroots production community. This democratization was in marked contrast to the barriers to entry of the high production cost, major label **DISCO** styles that preceded house. The name derives from the Chicago nightclub "The Warehouse" – local stores would mark records "As played at The Warehouse." See also **ACID HOUSE**.

how very *interjection* Dryly sarcastic expression indicating that the speaker would dearly like to feign enthusiasm about the subject under discussion but is unable to locate a suitable polite adjective due to it being asinine, absurd, pretentious, etc. beyond words. *"Probably just row on out to the middle of a lake. Bring along my sax, some tequila, and some Bach." "How very." (From "Heathers," 1989.)*

huey *verb* See **RALPH**.

hunk *noun* An attractive, tall, muscular male. Derives from the word's original meaning as a large slab or block of something. *"My Gohd! What a hunk! Oh, God, check out those pecs." (From "Valley Girl," 1983.)*

hype *noun* Excitement, buzz, drama. Often used with either positive or negative connotation in relation to marketing and entertainment. Also "hype man," a **RAP**per tasked with backing up the lead artist with vocal emphasis and energizing the audience. *"I don't want this chump to come over here with all that hype, trying to make us look bad." (From "Rocky IV," 1985.)*

icy *adjective* Extremely **COOL**.

I kid you not *phrase* Assertion that one is serious, despite any appearance to the contrary ("I'm not kidding you"). Originally popularized as the catchphrase of "The Tonight Show"[1] host Jack Paar in the late 1950s, the phrase enjoyed a resurgence in the '80s (particularly among **YUPPIES**). *"It's the most definitive Dvořák! You'll like it, I kid you not." (From "Peggy Sue Got Married," 1986.)*

I know you are, but what am I? *phrase* Childish all-purpose retort to any insult. It's important to get this one the right way round; many a schoolyard rejoinder has been embarrassingly spoiled by a hastily uttered "I know I am, but what are you?" *"I know you are, but what am I, infinity!" (From "Pee-wee's Big Adventure," 1985.)*

illin' *noun* Behaving in a crazy, angry, or otherwise objectionable manner. *"Don't be illin', I'm just chillin.'" (From "Heartbreak Ridge," 1986.)*

I'm so sure *phrase* **"I'm SO sherr"** Drippingly sarcastic statement usually accompanied by a theatrical roll of the eyes or even the whole head, indicating that the only thing the speaker is sure about is that her interlocutor is a liar and/or jackass.

in a New York minute *phrase* Rapidly. The general assumption is that things happen quickly in New York. The specific reference, according to Johnny Carson,[2] is to the infinitesimal slice of nanotime between a traffic light turning green and the driver behind you honking his horn in that fair city. Roughly a quarter of a second, in practice (see Fig. 7). *"I could kick your ass off this hill in a New York minute." (From "Dirty Rotten Scoundrels," 1988.)*

---

1. "Tonight Starring Jack Paar," as the title was styled at the time.
2. As reported by William Safire in "New York Times" magazine's "On Language" column of the October 19, 1986 issue (section 6, page 12).

Fig. 7: New York Minute Calculation

1 New York Minute (NYMp[††]) = 0.25521840719 seconds
(or 0.00425364012 standard minutes)

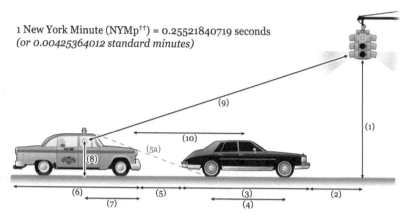

(1) Height of traffic light above road bed: 216" (548.64cm) (approx.)
(2) Pedestrian crosswalk width: 78" (198.12cm) (min.)*
(3) 1980 Cadillac Seville 4-door sedan total length: $204^{4/5}$" (520.19cm)
(4) " " " " wheelbase: 114" (289.56cm)
(5) Recommended safe red-light stopping distance: 68" (172.72cm) (approx.) **
(5a) Aft vehicle driver line of sight (est.) – see **
(6) Checker model A8 total length: $199^{1/2}$" (506.73cm)
(7) Distance between front of aft vehicle and driver: $88^{2/5}$" (224.54cm) (approx.)
(8) Distance between road bed and aft vehicle driver's head: 48" (121.92cm) (approx.)
(9) Distance of light traveled (hypotenuse/hyp): $\sqrt{((1) - (8))^2 + ((2)+(3)+(5)+(7))^2}$ = $470^{1/4}$" (1,194.44cm)
(10) Distance of sound traveled betwen aft vehicle horn and fore vehicle driver (horntravel/ht): 178.5" (453.39cm)

Constant: speed of light (c): $11,802,852,67^{33/200}$"/sec. (29,979,245,800 cm/s)
Constant: speed of sound (sos): $13503^{47/50}$"/sec. (34,300 cm/s)

Experimental variable: light change reaction time (lcrt): 0.242s ***

Therefore:

NYM actual[†] (NYMa) = ((hyp / c) = 39.84ns) + lcrt = 0.24200003984s
NYM perceived[††] (NYMp) = NYMa + ((ht / sos) = 0.01321836735s) = 0.25521840719s

* N.Y. State Dept. of Transportation Highway Design Manual, Ch. 18, Pedestrian Facility Design (p. 18-45).
** Ability to see rear tires of vehicle ahead.
*** Author experiment: https://faculty.washington.edu/chudler/java/redgreen.html
† Time elapsed between light change and aft vehicle driver depressing horn actuator.
†† Time elapsed between light change and fore vehicle driver hearing aft vehicle's horn.

Indian burn *noun* Form of mild, commonplace torture: to grab the victim's wrist or forearm firmly with both hands and twist vigorously in opposite directions with each hand. A favorite of school bullies everywhere. See also **MELVIN**. *"He reached up to trap her hands, and she gave her an Indian burn." (From "Thunder High" by Linda Shaw, 1988.)*

insane *adjective* See **OUTRAGEOUS**.

intense *adjective* **"in-TENSE!"** Exciting, exhilarating, terrifying. *"Wow! That was intense!" (From "Repo Man," 1984.)*

in your dreams *phrase* Dismissive retort indicating that whatever has just been suggested would never happen in reality. *"How dare you* *speak that way about my wife?" "Your wife? In your dreams!" "For real." (From "Cocktail," 1988.)*

isn't that special? *phrase*   Rhetorical question employed by Saturday Night Live[1] character The Church Lady (played by Dana Carvey) in response to hearing something absurd, nonsensical, stupid, or otherwise to be politely ignored. Similar to the popular Southern expression "Bless your heart!" – implying that the subject is a **DIPSHIT** but can't help it. *"There's so much that we aren't told about [...] the fact that Hitler's brain is being kept alive in Paraguay." "Well, isn't that special?" (From "Saturday Night Live," February 27, 1988.)*

it's been real *phrase*   Somewhat opaque expression of farewell, ostensibly stating that the time spent has been enjoyable, but sometimes used critically to suggest that the experience has been a little too real or, conversely, quite surreal, or to ruefully imply that reality is overrated. *"See ya, Doc." [...] "Yes, Doctor. It's been real." (From "The 'Burbs," 1989.)*

---

1. See also **YEAH, THAT'S THE TICKET.**

jack *verb* To steal, usually with threats and/or violence, or at least a little drama (from "hijack").

jacked *adjective* Intoxicated, high, excited, crazy, hyper. Also "jacked up." *"You sell to the kids. [...] You get 'em good and jacked up for three hours, so that by ten o'clock, they're ripping the house apart." (From "Big," 1988.)*

jam *verb* To leave, particularly in a hurry. *"You never know when you may have to jam." (From "The Breakfast Club," 1985.)*

jams *noun* Music, songs. From early 20th-century musician slang, referring to performance in an impromptu group, usually with an emphasis on improvisation. *(Ref. "I'm the Man" by Anthrax, 1987.)*

jam, the *noun* See PUMP UP THE JAM.

JAP *noun* "Jewish-American Princess," a pejorative epithet for the archetypal spoiled, solipsistic, rich girl; something of an East Coast counterweight to the Californian VALLEY GIRL stereotype. *(Ref. "JAP Rap" by 2 Live Jews, 1990.)*

jazzed *adjective* PSYCHED.

jazz, on the *adjective* To be not only PSYCHED and focused on the mission at hand, but in complete resonant harmony with the rhythm of the moment. This allows one to perform dazzling, apparently miraculous feats of inspired improvisation. *"What's up?" "He's on the jazz, man. He's on the jazz." (From the "The A-Team" episode "Black Day at Bad Rock," 1983.)*

Jel *noun* An idiot or DOOFUS. Abbreviation of "Jell-O brain."

jerk *noun* A selfish, annoying person; a DICK. *"Hey, you guys! You gotta let me in!" "Jerk alert!" (From "The Goonies," 1985.)*

jet *verb* To leave rapidly.

Joanie *noun* Pejorative VALLEY GIRL appellation for a square, unCOOL young female. After Joanie Cunningham, the all-American-gal character on the TV show "Happy Days."

jock *noun* A student athlete. Portrayed (individually or as a group) as the bullying, meat-headed antagonist in countless high school movies and TV shows. This is presumably because after college such sportsmen rarely go in for screenwriting as a career and thus wind up culturally underrepresented and unfairly maligned. History may be written by the winners but the same cannot be said of the entertainment industry's output. The term derives from the "jockstrap" or "groin guard" used in defense of the male genitalia when participating in contact sports, in which "jock" is a contraction of "jockey." *"Where the hell are we gonna live?" [...] "You're jocks. Go live in the gym." (From "Revenge of the Nerds," 1984.)*

joint, the *adjective* Rapper's slang, employed adjectivally: **CHOICE** or **COOL**. Also used (noun) in more mainstream idiom to mean a certain location; particularly a music venue (or disco, bar, etc.) or prison. *(Ref. "Shake Your Rump" by Beastie Boys, 1989.)*

jones *verb* To crave something. Originally (as a noun) much earlier slang for a drug habit. In the '80s (and thereafter) more commonly used hyperbolically to indicate a less intense desire, such as for a particular foodstuff.

joystick *noun* A game controller derived from aircraft controls. The joystick consists of a sturdy column connected at its lower end to a base containing numerous sensors which translate stick movement into electronic data, usually with one or more buttons on stick or base for initiating in-game actions. A common method of game control during the 1980s, particularly among home computer users (see **COMMODORE**), later decreasing in popularity in favor of the pad-type controllers popularized by manufacturers of third-generation consoles such as the Nintendo Entertainment System and Sega Master System, though retained in most arcade game cabinets. Etymology is uncertain, though most likely deriving from the surname of an early aviator and, presumably, its inventor. Possible originators are "George stick" (after British aviator Arthur Edward George, 1875–1951) or "Joyce stick" (after American aviator James Henry Joyce, 1888–1975), a likelier derivation. Also, predictably, a euphemism for the penis. *"If anything has to go, I'm glad it's my vision and not the old joystick, you know what I mean?" (From "Weekend at Bernie's," 1989.)*

juiced *adjective* Intoxicated, hyper, positively maniacal. Originally simply slang for "drunk," dating back to the 1940s. *"Those guys are more juiced up than that Ferrari." (From "The Cannonball Run," 1981.)*

kegger *noun* A beer-based social gathering, generally featuring one or more kegs – pressurized stainless steel beer barrels commonly available in several sizes from 1/6 bbl (one-sixth of a 31½-gallon standard barrel) to, preferably, ½ bbl. Unavoidably and eternally linked to the exuberantly overindulgent cultural milieu of the frat house. *"We're goin' to a kegger, and we'd like you to come, man." (From "Say Anything…," 1989.)*

kick-ass *adjective* Excellent, of superior quality. That which would kick the ass of the competition. *"You've won a victory for our way of life, my pride, my admiration and a kick-ass vacation." (From "Die Hard 2," 1990.)*

kicker *noun* Slightly more polite version of **SHITKICKER**.

kickin' *verb* Taking it easy, relaxing, **CHILL**ing out ("kicking back"). Also (adjective, from "kicking ass") cool, excellent. See also **KICK-ASS**. *"I'm kickin' it down in the garage." (From "Die Hard," 1989.)*

kicks *noun* Footwear, particularly sneakers. A popular slang term in the '80s but in subcultural use (including hobo and military slang) for many decades prior and since.

kill *adjective* Excellent, tremendous: used adjectivally "that was kill." Abbreviation of **KILLER**. **VALSPEAK**.

killer *adjective* Extraordinarily, shockingly excellent. Often simply used as an exclamation. *"Watch this, it's killer!" (From "Cobra," 1986.)*

killer app *noun* An application that, by taking advantage of new advances in hardware technology, enables a user to accomplish something previously impossible and therefore ensures that either it or its host computer system is the only real choice for the consumer, thus "killing" the competition. The word "app"/"application" is used primarily to refer to a specific piece of software, but can also be used in reference to a general area of activity to which a computer may be applied, for example, "High-quality OCR will be the next killer app." *"Right now, the pundits are pinning their dreams on OS/2, hoping upon hope that it will be the key to the next killer app." (From "PC" magazine, July 1989.)*

k-rad *adjective* **BBS** slang meaning "extremely **COOL**." "Rad" is a shortened **RADICAL** and "K" derives from the "Kilo-" prefix, indicating multiplication by one thousand (okay, or 1,024 in binary, wise guy). By the early 1990s the term had come to be used sarcastically, imitating the overenthusiasm of the newbie.

kvetchy *adjective* Of a person, to be a habitual complainer; whiny. From the Yiddish "kvetchn," to pinch. *"Laura Nyro, kvetchy singer-song-writer." (From "Spy" magazine's "Who's No Longer Who" column, April 1988.)*

lame *adjective* Weak, styleless, guileless, inelegant, half-assed, dumb. Particularly of a person or thing attempting to appear **COOL, HIP, FRESH**, with-it, but failing miserably. An ancient word with variations throughout European languages. *"This party's lame, Max!" (From "Weird Science," 1985.)*

lame-o *noun* **"lame-oh"** One who is **LAME**. *"Ricky! Get this lame-o out of your yard!" (From "The 'Burbs," 1989.)*

later days *phrase* Goodbye, good fortune. Shortening of "Later days and better lays."

legit *adjective* Legitimate: used for decades in the sense of trustworthy or non-criminal, but with an expanded reference in the '80s, to additionally mean **COOL, AWESOME**. *"Now, if she looks legit, send her to the alley behind the Kozy Kat Klub at 2AM tonight." (From "The A-Team" episode "Mexican Slayride," 1983.)*

like *various* Possibly the most versatile word in 1980s slang and consequently the most meaningless. In its most disparaged '80s usage "like" can be employed as a simple filler (also known as a filled pause, hesitation marker, or planner); something one says to buy time while figuring out what to say next, as in "Well ... Like ... Hello!" Likewise, but with a little more meaning, "like" can be used as a hedge (in the same sense as "hedge your bets"): a word or phrase employed with some ostensible meaning but with the primary purpose of toning down the sense or ameliorating the negative impact of what is subsequently said. Hedges are often used for reasons of politeness, trepidation, uncertainty, etc. For example, "Are you, like, really sure that's, like, safe?" "Like" can also be a discourse marker; a vaguely defined linguistic class that is generally applied to any nonsyntactic oral utterance that has no concrete semantic meaning but which may serve to connect, compare, or separate other concepts. For example, "There's this girl, like, dancing on stage." In somewhat[1] different usage, "like" is also frequently employed as a conversational quotative; a verbal indicator that what follows is quoted speech. For example, "I was like, 'Who do you think you're talking to?'" This usage also indicates that what follows the "like" may be a general imitative impression and not necessarily an exact representation. "Like" can also add emphasis; for example, "I picked up the phone and it was, like, her!" implies "it was actually, really

---

1. That was a "hedge"; the contrast between these various uses is hardly distinct.

her!" These colloquial uses can be traced back to the jazz/beat slang of the 1950s. *(Ref. "Valley Girl" by Frank Zappa, 1982.)*

limp-dick *noun* A weak, spineless, unimpressive, pathetic object. Usually indicating a person, but applicable to any ineffectual thing. Also used adjectivally, as in the citation. *"And to the limp-dick reporter it looks like the deputies are down on the asphalt giving CPR to the suspect." (From "Colors" by Kirk Mitchell and Joel Norst, 1988.)*

locking *noun* See **POPPING AND LOCKING**.

loogie *noun* An unpleasant mixture of saliva and phlegm, expectorated and employed in an antisocial manner. *"It's always fun to hock a loogie at the body of Quality Fiction." (From "Witness" journal, 1989.)*

major *adjective* Serious, extreme. Usually used straight, sometimes sarcastically, as in the citation. *"Maybe you could just stand there with me and my dudes and just be you, and –" "Sounds major." (From "Sixteen Candles," 1984.)*

majorly *adverb* Extremely, to a great degree. *"Isn't that majorly freaky? I mean is [your home] majorly big or what?" (From "Two Roads to Dodge City" by Adam Nicolson, 1987.)*

make me barf *interjection* See **BARF ME OUT**.

make my day *phrase* See **GO AHEAD, MAKE MY DAY**.

mall chick *noun* A girl who hangs out at the mall frequently. Distinct from the **MALL RAT** in that she might actually buy something from time to time.

mall maggot *noun* A form of "life" even lower than the **MALL RAT**.

mall rat *noun* A teen of either sex who habitually infests the local mall on account of having nothing better, or indeed at all, to do. Mall rats generally lurk in small groups and tend to be surly and depressive, often with good reason due to the acne, pale skin, limp greasy hair, etc., caused by a lack of exposure to sunlight and a diet consisting almost entirely of processed plasti-cheese and Slush Puppies. *"Ten years ago a 'mall rat' was a kid with stringy hair and a boom box who hung out in shopping plazas playing video games." (From "Take this Exit: Rediscovering the Iowa Landscape" by Robert F. Sayre, 1989.)*

man, the *noun* Any authority figure, in the abstract. In a distinct switch from its earlier usage as a term of reluctantly respectful enmity (as in "Stick it to the man!") in the 1980s "the man" tended to feature more in exclamations of praise – "You're the man!" "He's the man!" – indicating that the person in question was a fellow of rare accomplishments, deserving deference. *"You're the man! You're the man! Easy game! Eeeasy game!" (From "Bull Durham," 1988.)*

MASH *noun* Acronym: "Mansion, Apartment, Shack, House." A game popular among young girls, purportedly capable of divining one's future residence and requiring only a pencil, paper, and suspension of disbelief. Also (verb, lowercase) to make out with someone, as in "mash faces."

mass *adjective* A large quantity of, as in "We've got mass work to do." Also (adverb) used in place of "very," as in "That was mass cool."

maximum brilliant *adjective* Fantastic, wonderful. Due to the extravagant hyperbole, often used with what amounts to unintentional sarcasm. *"Like, he was maximum brilliant and they were, well, like, airheads." (From "The Official Computer Hater's Handbook" by DJ Arneson, 1983.)*

max out *verb* To do something to its upper limit. Also to abuse a credit card. See also **TO THE MAX**. *"I mean, he was maxed out on R&D when his goober head melvin friends were into M&Ms." (From "The Official Computer Hater's Handbook" by DJ Arneson, 1983.)*

McFly *interjection* See **HELLO, McFLY?**

McJob *noun* Derisive term for any lowly, poorly paid, unskilled job offering little satisfaction or potential for advancement, taken only out of economic necessity where no alternative is available. Derives from global fast-food restaurant franchise McDonald's much-parodied habit of adding the Scottish patronymic prefix to every aspect of its business. *"The Fast-Food Factories: McJobs Are Bad for Kids" (From "Washington Post," August 1986.)*

meat puppet *noun* A person of limited intelligence who thoughtlessly does whatever he or she is told. *"Meat puppet: Backstage lingo for none-too-bright TV-news anchorman." (From "Newsweek" magazine, 1989.)*

mega *adjective* Extremely good, or just extreme. Derives from the metric unit prefix indicating ten to the power of six (a factor of one million), which itself derives from the ancient Greek for "great." Often used as an intensifying prefix, as in the cited lyrics' "mega-prick" and **MEGABITCH**. *(Ref. "Black and Huge" by GWAR, 1990.)*

megabitch *noun* A highly intensified "bitch": one who has apparently chosen bitchery as her one true calling in life. See also **MEGA**. *"The boss of Twin Peaks's biggest industry, a lumber mill, is neither your crisp WASP tycoon with a well-groomed head of white shoe polish nor your aging, raven-haired megabitch but a young, beautiful, sweet Chinese woman." (From "The Connoisseur" magazine, 1989.)*

meltdown *noun* An explosive episode of extreme emotional outburst or more general breakdown. A linguistic reflection of lingering concern over nuclear power after the Three Mile Island accident in 1979 and the Chernobyl disaster seven years later.

melvin *noun* To sharply yank a victim's underwear upwards from the front (in contrast to a wedgie, which is from the rear).[1] This results in a condition in which the victim appears to be wearing his shirt tucked into his underwear, the habit of a true **DORK**. A highly dangerous prank that should not be attempted by anyone for any reason, due to the danger of testicular damage. The name Melvin has long been considered inherently humorous, as in the dialog from the cover of Mad Magazine #1 (1953): "That thing! That slithering blob coming toward us!" "What is it?" "It's Melvin!" See also the citation for **MAX OUT** for an example of the term's use as a derogatory epithet. Melvins have been the subject of at least one US District Court case; Pascual v.

---

1. This distinction is disputed by some, who claim that "melvin" and "wedgie" are entirely synonymous.

MENTAL

Anchor Advanced Products, Inc., 819 F. Supp. 728 (1993) relates the cautionary tale of "melvin activities" at a Morristown, TN, precision molded plastic products firm in the late 1980s. *"I can't believe we just melvined Death!" (From "Bill and Ted's Bogus Journey," 1991.)*

Fig. 8: Melvin Procedure

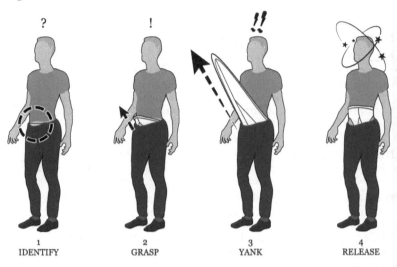

1	2	3	4
IDENTIFY	GRASP	YANK	RELEASE

DANGER: DO NOT TRY THIS AT HOME OR ANYWHERE ELSE.

mental *adjective* Acting crazy, insane. *"Your father has finally gone completely mental." (From "A Fish Called Wanda," 1988.)*

metal *noun* see **HEAVY METAL**.

metalhead *noun* See **HEADBANGER**.

Miller time *noun* Time of day at which it is appropriate and acceptable to enjoy a cold beer in a celebratory manner, having achieved something of note or at least finished the day's work. From the long-running advertising slogan for Miller High Life. *"Hey, we have the tools, we have the talent!" "It's Miller time!" (From "Ghostbusters," 1984.)*

mind frame *noun* A metaphorical aperture through which one's psyche subjectively perceives the objective universe, like an observer looking out through the window of a building. The size of the window and the panorama it reveals determines the quantity and quality of sense data the observer can receive and process, and therefore influences the degree to which the observer's world view or Weltanschauung achieves conformity with true reality. Thus, the intended implication is usually that this rigid structure blocks us from seeing or considering unexplored alternatives or opportunities. *"So is it something within our own institutional mind frame that leads us to believ* *that we deal with defectors who are associated with intelligence activities and disregard the others?" (From "Federal Government's Handling of Soviet and Communist Bloc Defectors" by the Permanent Subcommittee of Investigations of the Committee on Governmental Affairs, US Senate, October 1987.)*

mint *adjective* Fresh, cool, awesome. From the phrase "in mint condition." Also "minty."

mix tape *noun* A selection of songs mixed by a DJ and distributed on cassette **TAPE**. The term is also used to describe a collection of songs recorded onto one tape from another. Though no "mixing" in the musical sense is involved in this usage, the songs themselves are typically from a mix of artists (see Fig. 12 on page 114). This was usually accomplished using a double cassette deck of the type commonly found in **BOOMBOX**es and home entertainment systems of the period. Such mix tapes would often be made for and gifted to current or prospective romantic partners in order to gently let them know what kind of a person they're dealing with.

mocktail *noun* A mixed drink exhibiting all the outward attributes associated with a cocktail but cruelly containing no alcohol at all: a mock cocktail. See also **DECAF**. *"The mocktail is not a new idea, but the expanding market for alternatives to alcoholic beverages is new." (From "Core Concepts in Health" by Paul M. Insel and Walton T. Roth, 1988.)*

moded *verb* To be embarrassed or humiliated by having been outclassed, outmaneuvered, or otherwise defeated in some aspect of daily life. Predominantly California slang, possibly deriving from "outmoded." Alternatively spelled "moted," perhaps from "demoted," or "molded," as in to be rendered moldy.

molded *verb* See **MODED**.

mommy track *noun* In a positive sense, a workplace arrangement or career path for women who wish to balance work with motherhood. In a negative sense, punishment for same. By analogy with and as an alternative to "the fast track." *"Schwartz endorsed what the media quickly labeled 'the mommy track' [...] as the ideal slow lane for post-superwomen." (From "Mother Jones" magazine, June 1989.)*

mondo *adjective* Great, cool, tremendous either in quality or size. Derives from the "mondo" genre of low-budget, low-quality, exploitation/shockumentary film. The genre takes its name from the first well-known example, "Mondo Cane" (1962), the title being Italian for "(A) Dog's World." Also used as an adverb, as in "It was mondo weird."

money talks and bullshit walks *phrase* Pithy reminder that noble words aren't worth the paper they're written on if they're not backed up by the cold, hard stuff, and that anyone not willing to put his money where his mouth should be ignored. The phrase was unintentionally popularized by Rep. Michael "Ozzie" Myers in 1979, who was covertly taped saying it while accepting a bribe as part of the FBI's Abscam sheik-down, an occurrence humorously referenced by Rep. Raymond F Lederer (who was also implicated and convicted) in the citation. *"Another Congressman from Philly. He's a friend of mine. He says* *money talks and bullshit walks." (From "House Reports: Nos. 107–157," United States Congressional Serial Set, 1981.)*

moonwalk *noun, verb* Dance move popularized by Michael Jackson, which when done skillfully creates the optical illusion that the dancer is walking forward while in fact moving backward. Previously known among poppers and lockers (see **POPPING AND LOCKING**) as "the backslide." The latter is a more appropriate name, since nothing about the move visually suggests walking on the moon, whose comparatively low gravity forces a long, slow, bouncing stride. Also (verb) the act of performing the dance, as in the citation. *"I will moonwalk all up and down your ass." (From "Eddie Murphy Raw," 1987.)*

mosh *verb* To dance in a vigorous, violent, indiscriminately thrashing fashion, usually to live **HEAVY METAL**, **PUNK**, or **HARDCORE** music. Also known, with some distinctions relevant only to the connoisseur, as "slamdancing" (see **SLAMDANCE**). Originally "mash."

most definitely *adverb* An emphatic affirmative. Standard English rendered slang by virtue of emphasis.

most triumphant *adjective* Excellent, good, deserving of praise. An example of the deliberately old-fashioned, ornate, hyperbolic demotic phraseology prevalent at the time. *"Will you go to the prom with us in San Dimas? We will have a most triumphant time." (From "Bill & Ted's Excellent Adventure," 1989.)*

motor *verb* To get going, leave, make tracks. Slightly **YUPPIE**ish phrase. *"Well, great pâté, but I'm gonna have to motor if I wanna be ready for that funeral." (From "Heathers," 1989.)*

motor mouth *noun* A monologist who has not grasped the two-way nature of conversation, prone to drone on interminably about some pet subject or reminiscence. Utterly exhausting to be around. *"If you've hit on the party wallflower, you're in good shape, but there's the opposite extreme, the Motor Mouth," (From "Orange Coast" magazine, December 1989.)*

mouth-breather *noun* A vacant, empty-headed specimen; a knucklehead. One who has not yet learned to appreciate the benefits of nasal respiration and consequently walks around with his or her lower mandible hanging open, drooling.

much *adverb* Suffixed adverbially to the preceding word in order to inquire whether a person does that thing a lot, greatly exhibits the relevant quality, etc. (usually sarcastically). For example, "Jealous much?" would in standard English be "Are you very jealous?" *"God, Veronica, drool much? His name is Jason Dean." (From "Heathers," 1989.)*

multitask *verb* Of a computer system, to enable a user to have multiple programs open and accessible at the same time. Of a human, to inattentively mismanage multiple assignments at once, saving time over the traditional approach of ensuring one project is completely botched before moving on to the next. *"Although some people continue to question whether multitasking is really necessary on a single-user computer, users are definitely ready for multitasking and can benefit from it. (From "Programming Windows" by Charles Petzold, 1988.)*

mung *verb* To render data (in large amounts, of immense importance, or both) unreadable, irreparably damaged, or otherwise worthless, by means of a computer. This usually occurs due to the operator or programmer's human error or, debatably, is ascribable to the machine's innate malevolence. By the early 1980s computers were well-established in the corporate world; consequently, their capacity and apparent proclivity for large-scale automated destruction was already infamous. As one "Washington Post" article[1] put it, "The 'enemies list' of computers seems endless. [...] For a few dollars you can buy a plaque that reads 'To err is human – to really foul things up requires a computer.'" *"Note that the System only mungs things maliciously (this is a consequence of Murphy's Law)." (From "The Hacker's Dictionary," 1983 edition.)*

mutant *noun* A **WEIRDO**; one who is apparently genetically abnormal and is consequently shunned by the herd. The popularity of this scientific term was mainly due to its frequent use in movies and television to conveniently explain where monsters come from (see **CHUD**). *"My best friend's conversing with a mutant, and I'm curious." (From "Pretty in Pink," 1986.)*

my way or the highway *phrase* Expression indicating that the speaker will not tolerate subordinates' deviation from his or her methods and that anyone who can't handle that fact is welcome to get lost. *"I'm telling you straight, it's my way or the highway. So anybody wants to walk, do it now." (From "Roadhouse," 1989.)*

---

1. "Coping: Computers and You" by Carol Krucoff, September 23, 1980.

nads *noun* The testicles. Abbreviation of "gonads." *"Moe-Lay*[1] *really pumps my nads." (From "The Breakfast Club," 1985.)*

narbo *noun* Canadian dialect for an uncool person or thing.

narc *noun* Originally a narcotics agent or vice cop, usually undercover. In the 1980s the term's meaning expanded to encompass an informer, snitch, or tale-teller in any relevant setting, such as a school or workplace. Also used as a verb, as in "to narc on someone." Also an ultraviolent 1988 arcade game which attracted significant controversy for its depiction of graphic bloodshed and the absurdity of having a giant disembodied head **SPORT**ing a ten-foot-wide Panama hat as an end boss.

nards *noun* The testicles. Possibly related to **NADS** or alternatively an abbreviation of "innards." *"It was boss! I saw Dracula! And I kicked Wolfman in the nards!" (From "The Monster Squad," 1987.)*

negaholic *noun* One who is psychologically addicted to persistent negative behavior such as complaining, fault-finding criticism, and general pessimism. A wet blanket. *"Instead of saying you complain too much, you're a negaholic who needs to learn self-empowerment." (From "Mademoiselle" magazine, 1989.)*

nerd *noun* A socially underdeveloped, square, unfashionable, studious person. Not necessarily unpopular per se – nerds would tend to agglomerate in small, mutually unthreatening groups – but distinctly disesteemed by those who would consider themselves of superior status in the social hierarchy. Far from being the somewhat backhanded but often genuine compliment "nerd" implies today the life of an '80s nerd was not to be viewed in any sort of positive light, except in revenge fantasies dreamed up by downtrodden, underpaid Hollywood screenwriters (see **JOCK**). The most appealing etymological origin theory is that "knurd," being "drunk" backwards and therefore (via a sort of linguistic half-logic) its inverse, is a sober non-drinker who would rather study than party. Also ("Nerds") a colorful lumpy, tongue-staining "tiny tangy crunchy candy" popular from 1983 (see also **DWEEB**). *"It says, 'Nerds, get out.'" "What's a nerd?" "We are." (From "Revenge of the Nerds," 1984.)*

network *verb* **YUPPIE** slang for the consumption of alcohol. Specifically, of a lower-level or beginner yuppie, to go to parties or other events in the hope of meeting and impressing higher-ranking yuppies in a position to further his or her career goals. The trouble

---

1. Lunkheaded mispronunciation of "Molière."

with this approach as a method of actually achieving anything other than the acquisition of a persistent substance abuse problem is that ninety percent of the other attendees have exactly the same plan, while the remaining ten percent are there to prey upon the ambitious, naive majority in one way or another. *"Come on, Brad, it'll be fun. And it's never too soon to start networking." (From "Soul Man," 1986.)*

new jack *adjective* Descriptive of a neophyte in any given society, milieu, or scene (from prison slang). Also an original, fresh artistic concept. Related to "new jack swing," a late '80s fusion of **HIP HOP** and R&B. *(Ref. "You Gots to Chill" by EPMD, 1988.)*

new romantic *noun* A UK-origin musical and fashion movement, under the umbrella of **NEW WAVE**. New romantic bands such as Spandau Ballet (house band of the **BLITZ** club), Duran Duran, Visage, Adam and the Ants, Culture Club, and many others, musically tended toward the synthpop end of the new wave spectrum, with a focus on atmospherics and emotion. Perhaps more importantly, they derived stylistic and thematic inspiration from 1970s glam rock, 1920s–30s Weimar cabaret culture and, as the movement's name suggests, 18th–19th-century literary romanticism. These bands achieved success as part of the "second British invasion" due mainly to their emphasis on visual style ensuring heavy MTV rotation. Boy George, singer of Culture Club, even starred as himself in an episode of "The A-Team" (season 4, episode 16: "Cowboy George," February 11, 1986). *"Right, that's it." [Opens van door.] "I'm getting out here if we're anything to do with the new romantics." (From "The Comic Strip Presents..." episode "Bad News Tour," 1983.)*

new wave *noun* A term described by the "New Rolling Stone Encyclopedia of Rock" as "virtually meaningless," but generally applied to several genres of popular music that originated from and grew up alongside the initially more popular **PUNK** movement in the mid- to late 1970s. Being partially a reaction to the perceived excesses of punk, new wave survived that trend's shrinking popularity as the '80s progressed, moving firmly into the chart mainstream. New wave acts tended to embrace punk's anti-corporatism and "do it yourself" ethic, but eschewed its abrasive, raucous aesthetic and politically charged subject matter in favor of more accessible pop styles and tropes. Prototypical new wave bands include late '70s CBGB favorites Television and Talking Heads, but the term is also applied to later synth-pop bands, particularly those of the MTV-led "second British invasion" (see **NEW ROMANTIC**) of the early to mid-1980s such as Duran Duran and their ilk, as well as coeval homegrown oddities like Devo. Artists like The Pretenders and Ramones muddied the waters between new wave on the one hand and rock and punk respectively on the other. *(Ref. "It's Still Rock and Roll To Me" by Billy Joel, 1980.)*

new-waver *noun* Specifically, one involved in the **NEW WAVE** scene, but broadly any young person with a non-mainstream appearance. *"Here's the young new-waver we've all heard so much about." (From "Repo Man," 1984.)*

New York minute *noun* See **IN A NEW YORK MINUTE**.

nice head *phrase* Sarcastic non-compliment expressing one's dissatisfaction with the target's hairdo (hairdon't).

nice play, Shakespeare *phrase* Reaction to another person's ill-considered, insensitive, or boneheaded move, particularly when it backfires spectacularly. A deliberate conflation of two senses of the word "play," referring to both a deliberate, considered action in sports or other competition and a piece of narrative performance. The latter sense is epitomized by the work of William Shakespeare, the Bard of Avon, widely considered the world's greatest dramatist and thus someone to whom it is amusing to compare the muttonhead in question.

NIMBY *noun* Acronym for "Not In My Back Yard." Alludes to the typical homeowner's attitude that debatably necessary but definitely unpleasant public or private facilities are all well and good but should be built somewhere other than his or her neighborhood (or upwind thereof). Primarily used as a critical term for one expressing such thoughts. *"NIMBY syndrome affects the siting of prisons, airports, mental health centers, power plants, landfills, and hazardous waste facilities." (From "Forum for Applied Research and Public Policy" journal, 1987.)*

no biggie *interjection, noun* No big deal; no problem, forget about it. *"The point is that everyone has a bad dream once in a while. It's no biggie." (From "A Nightmare on Elm Street," 1984.)*

no can do *phrase* Bizarre muddling or simplification of "I can't do that." Much favored by **YUPPIE**s as an indication that the speaker is far too busy to invest the time required to utter the complete phrase. Originated in Chinese Pidgin English of the 17th–19th centuries, also known as Chinese Coastal English, explaining its grammatical oddity. *(Ref. "I Can't Go for That (No Can Do)" by Hall & Oates, 1981.)*

no doubt *adverb, interjection* Definitely, **FOR SURE**. As an interjection, expression of unambiguous agreement. *"Veronica's into his act, no doubt." (From "Heathers," 1989.)*

no doy *interjection* See **DOY**.

no duh *interjection* See **DOY, DUH**.

no fake *interjection* For real, no fooling, **I KID YOU NOT**.

noid *noun* A **NERD**. In fact, simply the word "nerd" pronounced with a nasal, **GEEK**y accent. "The Noid" was a highly popular advertising anti-mascot employed by Domino's Pizza in TV spots from 1986. The outlandish, manic, pot-bellied, red-rabbit-suit-wearing claymation Noid was obsessed with finding ways to ruin home delivery pizza; ordering from Domino's was therefore presented as the only way diners could "Avoid the Noid." In 1989 a disturbed 23-year-old man named Kenneth Lamar Noid, believing the pizza company was targeting him personally, took two employees hostage at a Domino's in Chamblee, GA. The situation was resolved peacefully, but the case caused significant negative publicity for Domino's, being a gift for pun-hungry newspaper headline writers; "Assault Suspect 'A-Noid

Over Use of Name" from the New Jersey "Courier-Post" being a typical example. *"Have you ever been frustrated because the Noid ruined your pizza? The Noid loves to ruin pizza." (Domino's pizza commercial, 1986.)*

no problemo *noun, interjection* Faux-Spanish embellishment of the standard "no problem," its coolness emphasizing that the subject under discussion is of only trifling difficulty. *"Mobility's good? No problem getting off the throw to second?" "No problemo." (From "Major League," 1989.)*

no shit, Sherlock *phrase* Rejoinder expressing the opinion that the previous speaker has said something blindingly obvious, invoking the great literary detective Sherlock Holmes. Sarcastically implies that only a sleuth equal to Holmes would be acute enough to arrive at such a startlingly unlikely but inspired conclusion as that which one's interlocutor has just bestowed upon one. See also **FUCK YOU, WATSON**. *"Look, all I'm saying is that we have to be careful." [...] "No shit, Sherlock!" (From "Dead Poets Society," 1989.)*

not even *interjection* A negatory reply indicating disagreement. Truncation of "not even slightly," "not even close," etc. This negation can itself be negated with the emphatic counter-riposte "Even!"

no way *interjection* Expression of surprised disbelief ("There's no way that could be true"). Often succinctly responded to with "**WAY**!" *"Trust you? You drive worse than Maureen." "No way!" [Car mounts pavement.] (From "Beverly Hills Cop II," 1987.)*

nowhere *adjective* Ignorant, unhip, naive, clueless. The opposite of "with it" – without it. *(Ref. "Hip to Be Square" by Huey Lewis and the News, 1986.)*

nuke *verb* To prepare something (food, ideally) in a microwave. Derives from the fact that microwaves work at a molecular level (by irritating the water molecules in food, vibrating them to cause friction and thus heat) and also that the electromagnetic radiation with which they accomplish this can easily be conflated with nuclear radiation. However, while nuclear radiation is strong enough to kick electrons out of atoms (known as "ionizing" radiation), microwave radiation is not (known as "non-ionizing" radiation) and is thus not dangerous in the same way. That said, you don't want your water molecules rubbed rapidly against each other, either. *"Oh, I like nuked food!" (From "Twins," 1988.)*

nutbar *noun* An eccentric person prone to outlandish or wild thoughts or behavior; a lunatic. From "nut," the early twentieth century idiom for a crazy person (itself deriving from the use of "nut" to mean the human head, via "head case") and referencing nut-containing chocolate bars. See also **FUCKNUT**. *"Moose wasn't just any nutbar. He was pure Hershey with nuts in his head." (From "Escape from the Glue Factory" by Joe Rosenblatt, 1985.)*

ohmigod *interjection* **"ohmy-GOHD"** **VAL**-ish exclamation of joy, surprise, disbelief, alarm, or any other emotion. Variation on the standard "Oh my God!" with all three words smushed together, the first two spliced into a single rushed syllable in order to make room for the long, drawn-out, emphatic third. *"Ohmigod! Ohmigod! It's not true! Julie Bennet promised me an angel and she delivered.'" (From "The Sisters" by Pat Booth, 1987.)*

old-school *adjective* Nostalgic reference to the past, when all things were simpler, better, cheaper, and more wholesome. Specifically, in discussion of a person or thing that exemplified or still exemplifies the values and methods of that golden era. The period of time to which the term is applied may be quite recent, depending on one's frame of reference. See also **BACK IN THE DAY**. *(Ref. "I'm Still No. 1" by Boogie Down Productions, 1988.)*

-o-rama *suffix* Suffix employed to spice up trade names, particularly those of places of entertainment, to imply impressive magnitude and scope (for example, "Bowl-O-Rama"). Consequently, often applied to any other word to indicate that there is a whole lot of (word) going on and indeed that the current situation is an archetypal exemplar or bountiful extravaganza of (word). Derives from the ancient Greek for "spectacle," as in "panorama." *"Lardass just sat back and enjoyed what he'd created. A complete and total barf-o-rama." (From "Stand by Me," 1986.)*

out *adjective* Unfashionable, yesterday's news, to be shunned: out of style. Also to be generally unacceptable or off the table. Also, as a verb, to reveal someone (usually a celebrity or politician) as being secretly gay; from "out of the closet."

outrageous *adjective* Hyperbolically excellent.

outta here *phrase* Predictive expression stating that a person is about to get gone. Usually in self-reference: "I'm outta here!" *"Point me toward the Big Bird to Paradise and I'm outta here...." (From "A Fine Madness" by Barbara Bretton, 1988.)*

out the door *phrase* To do something, or have something done to you, to the extent it causes one to leave the room or building. For example, **GROSS ME OUT THE DOOR** as an extension of **GROSS ME OUT**.

paninaro *noun*   Follower of an early 1980s Italian (originally Milanese) youth fashion phenomenon influenced by clothing and brands featured in American movies as well as Italian designer labels. Paninari generally embodied a carefree, optimistic attitude and outlook, in marked to contrast to many other youth tribes of that and previous eras, perhaps partially in appreciative mimicry of **YUPPIE** characters in those movies. The epithet derives from "panino," Italian for "bread," after their original meeting place, the "Al Panino" sandwich bar in Milan. *(Ref. "Paninaro" by Pet Shop Boys, 1986.)*

pants *verb* The prank or bullying act of pulling down another's pants around their ankles, exposing the victim's underwear to embarrassing public scrutiny and thus significantly undermining his dignity and gravitas. An awkward verb; present participle "pantsing," past participle "pantsed." One reason to wear a strong belt at all times. See also **MELVIN**. *"The riots seem to have been a series of fist fights and 'pantsing' escapades, not riots at all." (From "South Eastern Latin Americanist" journal, 1986.)*

parachute pants *noun* Clothing invented or adopted by early '80s **BREAKDANCER**s and fashioned from heavy-duty nylon – as used in the construction of parachute canopies – in order to withstand the rigors of the energetic dancing style. Not to be confused with the baggy, harem-style **HAMMER PANTS** of the late '80s and early '90s, though the term "parachute pants" is often misapplied to Hammer pants in popular culture. Parachute pants were fairly slim-fitting (though not too tight, to permit vigorous movement), similar to leather motorcycle pants, featuring numerous pockets and often equipped with contrast-colored zips and other accessories. Think "Thriller"-era Michael Jackson or imagine military pants as designed by Jean Paul Gaultier.

Fig. 9: Parachute vs. Hammer Pants

PANTS, PARACHUTE
(EARLY '80S)

PANTS, HAMMER
(LATE '80S)

parental unit *noun* A parent. First popularly used in the alien-themed Saturday Night Live "**CONEHEAD**s" sketches dating from 1977 as an imaginative and amusing example of the kind of cold, impersonal language employed by total **WEIRDO**s with no experience of human relationships. As in the citation, the term is also found in the professional literature of sociologists, though it is not clear whether this is intended as a deliberate joke or is an actual, real-world example of the kind of cold, impersonal language, etc. See also **RENTS**. *"If the socialization of children is the basic responsibility of individual parental units, then independent units of solidarity arise which can compete with the group for the member's loyalty." (From "Countercultural Communes: A Sociological Perspective" by Gilbert Zicklin, 1983.)*

party hearty *interjection, verb* JOCK-ish (or frat-ish) exhortation promoting exuberant, energetic enjoyment. To conscientiously apply oneself to fulfilling the latter injunction of "work hard, play hard." Often abbreviated simply to "Party!" or "Par-tay!" Also "Party on!" *"Hey, come on in and party hearty, dude persons!" (From "Sixteen Candles," 1984.)*

PC *adjective* See **POLITICALLY CORRECT**.

pecker *noun* A penis and, by extension, an annoying or despicable individual. See **DORK**. *"What are those damn freak pecker heads playing?" (From "The Blues Brothers," 1980.)*

peg *verb* To fold the hems of a pair of pants, particularly jeans, usually twice or more, in order to create a tightly-cuffed appearance. One of the many 1950s/'60s fashions to enjoy a resurgence in the '80s. Some sources suggest that the key to an ideal pegged cuff is to fold a vertical half-inch pleat at the bottom hem before folding the hem upwards, as this reduces the circumference of the opening and thus creates a neater look.

pencil in *verb* To set a provisional appointment subject to possible later change, the implication being that pencil can be erased from an appointment book if necessary ("I'll pencil you in for Wednesday afternoon"). Originally YUPPIE-talk, used as a minor power-play with the connotation that the subject is not important enough to deserve a firm commitment. Later in more general but slightly humorous use. *"[The] appointment book [is] the reference of last resort when trying to duck undesired invitations ('Gee, the soonest I can pencil you in is December 1989')." (From "Buzzwords: The Official MBA Dictionary" by Jim Fisk and Robert Barron, 1983.)*

penis breath *noun* Insult subtly insinuating that the target suffers from fellatio-induced halitosis. *"Maybe an elf or a leprechaun." "It was nothing like that, penis breath!" (From "E.T. the Extra-Terrestrial," 1982.)*

perfecto *interjection, adjective* Faux-Spanish embellishment of "perfect" with the same meaning but an added zing of stylishness. The term's use in slang may derive from the famously excellent "Perfecto" brand leather jacket made by Schott since the 1920s, itself named after founder Irving Schott's preferred type of cigar (a "perfecto" cigar bulges in the middle and tapers to the ends). *"I spent a shitload of money on her, and she's perfecto now." (From "Christine," 1983.)*

perp *noun* One who commits a crime; abbreviation of "perpetrator." Cop jargon, then street slang. A favorite of 1980s comic book sci-fi ubercop Judge Dredd. *"'A bad perp named Buddy Marlow.' 'Perp?' [...] 'Perpetrator. Doctors aren't the only ones who enjoy their slang.'" (from "Worth Any Risk" by Kathleen Korbel, 1987.)*

perp walk *noun* Deliberate pretrial public airing of a criminal suspect by police or other arresting agents for the benefit of the media, with the hotly denied but self-evident intention of implying guilt despite the legal presumption of innocence. See also **PERP**. *"The Second Circuit, while agreeing that a staged 'perp walk' violates the Fourth Amendment, held that the defendant police officer in the case was entitled to qualified immunity." (From "Almanac of the Federal Judiciary," 1984.)*

phat *adjective* Exceptionally good, with a connotation of richness and abundance. *(Ref. "Jane 3" by EPMD, 1990.)*

phreak *noun* A species of **HACKER** who specializes in accessing telephone systems in imaginative ways unintended by their designers. Also (verb) the action of so doing. Blend of "phone" and "freak." Much phreaking relied on replication of audio tones used by long-distance telephone systems for call routing; an inherently insecure system. *"A couple of years ago, one phreak racked up calls amounting to $100,000." (From "Computerworld" magazine, December 1989.)*

pig out *verb* To overeat voraciously in an entirely uninhibited, hedonistic manner. See also **SNARF**. *"Didn't you ever sit down to a big Christmas dinner and wish you didn't have to eat the turkey? Didn't you wish you could just pig out on the stuffing?" (From "Pig Out With Peg: Secrets from the Bundy Family Kitchen," 1990.)*

pillowcase *noun* A soft-headed, empty-minded person; a **DITZ**. *"So, what's the question?" [...] "I forgot." "Such a pillowcase." (From "Heathers," 1989.)*

poindexter *noun* See **DEXTER**.

poison pill *noun* An anti-hostile-takeover measure, enabling the purchase of stock at a highly discounted rate if any stockholder's position in the company exceeds a certain percentage of the total shares outstanding. Instated as a countermeasure to fend off corporate raiders. Also known as a "shareholder rights plan." See also **GREENMAIL**. *"You didn't expect a poison pill was gonna be running around the building." (From "Die Hard," 1988.)*

politically correct *adjective* Disparaging term sarcastically imitating the doublespeak employed by Soviet and other authoritarian regimes in their Orwellian attempts to eliminate dissent by shaping thought in a way that allows ideas to be viewed only in a right/wrong light. "Right" is, of course, defined by the Party. Often abbreviated to "PC." Originally satirically employed by left-wingers in gentle criticism of those in their own ranks seen as overly dogmatic, or in gentle mockery of one's own amusingly progressive behavior. Later employed by those on the right wing for the same purpose (i.e., in criticism of those on the left). The term has its origins in the 1970s but rose to wider cultural consciousness in the '80s. In the late '80s and early '90s it tended to lose its ironic connotations, being employed in earnest to express stern denunciation: "That's not politically correct!" Those who did this were usually unaware that the term originated as witty criticism of exactly that sort of imperious behavior. In a broader sense, the term refers to the tendency of all organizations and movements, to a greater or lesser extent, to develop a conceptual orthodoxy from which deviation is discouraged or even punished. *(Ref. "Please Let Me Be Your Third World Country" by The Bobs, 1987.)*

popping and locking *noun* **HIP HOP** dance styles often conflated but quite different from one another: "popping" refers to a wide range of generally robotic or rapid-fire moves performed using sudden and often spasmodic muscular contractions, whereas "locking" is a much looser and more fluid, expansive funk style characterized by crisp, rapid changes in direction and momentary freezes (i.e., "locking" the body in place). *"Who knows? With a little work you'll be poppin' and lockin' and breakin' in no time." (From "Breakin'," 1984.)*

Fig. 10: Popping vs. Locking

POPPING:

| TIGHT, HIGHLY CONTROLLED MOVES | AWKWARD, ROBOTIC POSES | JOINTS "POPPED" AT UNUSAL ANGLES |

LOCKING:

| LOOSER, FUNKIER MOVES | EXPANSIVE, FLUID GESTURES | POSES "LOCKED" FOR SEVERAL BEATS |

POSER

poser *noun* A pretentious person who seeks to give the false impression he or she belongs to some group or has attained a desirable level of success, fame, infamy, experience, etc. A boastful or flamboyant person in general. Also simply someone who tries to be **COOL** by adopting a physical attitude indicating nonchalance. *(Ref. "On the Loose" by Racer X, 1986.)*

posse *noun* A group of friends, specifically those on whom one can count for support in one way or another. Originally a posse was a group of regular citizens who agreed to help police or other agencies accomplish a specific task (such as capturing an outlaw or as part of a search party) on an ad hoc basis. Consequently one's posse is willing and, ideally, able to provide backup and ensure justice is done on one's behalf. The term also formed a key part of the viral "André the Giant Has a Posse" art sticker phenomenon in 1989, which later morphed into the iconic "OBEY" campaign. *(Ref. "Let's Get It Started" by MC Hammer, 1988.)*

POSSLQ *noun* **"pozzle-cue"** Acronym-initialism (a rare example of a single word containing both), meaning "Persons of Opposite Sex Sharing Living Quarters." First appeared in the 1980 US census form as a way of gauging unmarried cohabitation among couples (even though it is semantically equally applicable to married couples, it was not intended that way). The term's linguistic absurdity and puzzling meaning caused it to gain humorous semi-popular usage. As reported in the November 17, 1985 edition of the "Los Angeles Times": "'I am writing you because my wife and I are planning a party for my employees,' explains George A. Keplinger of Laguna Beach. 'When I verbally extended the invitation, I was asked if spouses were included. I responded in the affirmative and added that Posselques were invited also. Not one person knew what I meant.'" *"Doctors Sternin and Crane are proud to announce that they are now officially POSSLQs." [...] "You see, it's a little, uh, lovers' in-joke we picked up from a Census Bureau acronym." "Oh, I love those." (From the "Cheers" episode "Dinner at Eight-ish," 1987.)*

power dressing *noun* The wearing of clothing designed to project an image of capability, wealth, professionalism, and other such qualities as a method of gaining or maintaining status. Long the preserve of the male, starting in the late 1970s and becoming standard in the '80s professional women began to adopt office clothing emulating the masculine "power suit" and de-emphasizing traditionally feminine design. This was accomplished by means of attributes such as dark and/or high-contrast color schemes, sharp-angled tailoring, tapered waists, and above all large, squared-off shoulders. At least partially responsible for the rise of **BIG HAIR**, both fashions rocketed in popularity thanks to wildly trendy aspirational soap operas "Dallas" and "Dynasty." *"One magazine ran a piece on 'power dressing.' Another reported on how women were being advised to 'dress the trip to the top.'" (From "Fashion Power: The Meaning of Fashion in American Society" by Lauer & Lauer, 1981.)*

power lunch *noun* A midday meal, usually at a restaurant, at which (self-)important executives and other movers and shakers congregate for the laudable purpose of driving organizational progress but who are in reality usually inspired only to take long recuperative afternoon naps. See also **DO LUNCH, NETWORKING.** *"Gentlemen, that was a pretty poor showing for a power lunch." (From the "Cheers" episode "One Happy Chappy in a Snappy Serape," November 17, 1988.)*

power suit *noun* See **POWER DRESSING.**

preppy *noun, adjective* A person belonging to the subculture associated with elite, private, primarily northeastern "preparatory" or "college-preparatory" schools. Also, one who emulates the fashion and other customs of that subculture and those of the families who inundate such schools with their offspring. These institutions charge tuition fees, tend to be highly selective, and are often boarding establishments. They process inmates between the ages of 13 and 18, or thereabouts, with the goal of rendering them fit to take their places in the executive echelons of the nation. Preppy fashion had been a status symbol for many decades, particularly at the universities which prep school pupils would subsequently attend, but really took off in the mainstream with the 1980 publication of the massively popular "The Official Preppy Handbook," which sold over a million copies. With its connotations of old money, **WASP**ish high society, casual leisure and sporting lifestyles, preppy fashion was a perfect fit for the aspirational '80s, particularly for younger people looking for a stepping stone to **YUPPIE** status. This despite the fact that a yuppie is, by definition, a high-achieving professional with aspirations of upward mobility, whereas a true preppy is unlikely to have to work very hard for a living[1] and might look down on the yuppie as a bit of a try-hard arriviste, lacking savoir faire. Much of prep culture is more subtle than might be expected, relying on intergenerational inheritance of everything from wealth and values to clothing and vehicles. However, the most obvious classic preppy traits are to be found in its male attire: cuffed, pleated khakis, boat shoes or Bass Weejuns (without socks), button-down shirts (Oxford, extra points for Madras), pastel polos with whimsical insignia and popped collars, braided leather belts, tortoiseshell Ray Ban Wayfarers (see **SHADES**) on **CROAKIES**, and of course Shetland sweaters draped around the shoulders and tied like a scarf (a very practical style, undeserving of the ridicule it commonly attracts). As for feminine fashion, the "Official Preppy Handbook" authoritatively states: "Men and women dress as much alike as possible and clothes for either sex should deny specifics of gender." Also "preppie," "prep." *"Butt out, will you? Let's talk about the preppy with the Porsche." (From "Mystic Pizza," 1988.)*

primo *adjective* First-class, top-quality. Applicable to anything, but preponderantly employed in reference to recreational drugs, particu-

---

1. Nevertheless, such an individual may well choose to work regardless of need, the Protestant work ethic being a core preppy value. However, such hard work is likely to be somewhat covert as cultivation of an image of effortless success is also mandatory (see **COOL**).

larly marijuana. *"I tell you what, we're going to go out and cop some primo Cannabis sativa." (From "Club Paradise," 1986.)*

props *noun* Proper respect; the regard due someone on account of his or her achievements. *(Ref. "Jeff Waz on the Beat Box" by Jazzy Jeff & the Fresh Prince, 1989.)*

psych *interjection* Exclamation, usually uttered loudly in the face of the recipient, after having tricked him or her into believing something untrue. Also used in a less combative sense as an alternative to "only kidding!" The term is so often misspelled "sike" or "syke" that many will swear the error is in fact the correct spelling. This misconception likely arises due to the person having learned the slang term in early childhood, prior to becoming familiar with the phrase from which it derives: "psych out," to defeat someone in a mind game or unnerve an opponent before or during a contest. *(Ref. "Everything That Glitters (Ain't Always Gold)" by DJ Jazzy Jeff & The Fresh Prince, 1989.)*

psyched *adjective* To be **STOKED**, excited about something. Shortening of "psyched up," as in to be mentally prepared for the rigors of an athletic performance, etc. *"Come here, Foofie! Ah, Foofie, are you psyched? Are you ready?" (From "UHF," 1989.)*

psycho *noun* A mentally unbalanced person, particularly of a potentially dangerous type. Far from originating in the 1980s, the term goes back to at least the '40s and was widely used thereafter (as the eponymous 1960 Hitchcock movie attests). It nonetheless became a staple go-to insult in the '80s. For perhaps the first time it also gained a grudgingly respectful complimentary usage, being used not only in the sense of "someone not to be messed with" but also in reference to a person's obsessive, dedicated nature or preternatural skill in a given domain. Note that in the two citations from "Lethal Weapon" the term is used with two quite different meanings. In the first, it is a shortening of "psychopath," based on the popular belief in the dangerous nature of the disorder, whereas in the second it is a shortening of "psychological" (a "psycho pension" would be available to any **BURNOUT**, trauma sufferer, etc., and does not relate to psychopathy at all). *(1) "You'd be killing a cop." "Yeah, a psycho nut cop!" (2) "You're not trying to draw a psycho pension. You really are crazy." (From "Lethal Weapon," 1987.)*

pump up the jam *phrase* To party, **ROCK OUT**. Very late 1980s usage. Derives from the title of the massive hit dance single by Technotronic that peaked in the charts at the end of '89. *(Ref. "Pump up the Jam" by Technotronic, 1989.)*

punk *noun* Youth subcultural phenomenon originating in the mid-1970s and enjoying a resurgence in the early '80s, focused on various forms of punk rock music and punk fashion but also embracing a wide variety of artistic, literary, political, philosophical, and lifestyle concepts. In all of these, however, lay a fundamental do-it-yourself pro-individual, pro-local, anti-corporate, anti-collectivist philosophy that some might argue could be traced back to the hippie movement. This despite the marked differences in almost every other respect, as punk rejected the hippies almost as energetically as it rejected mainstream sociocultural values. Being partly a violently regurgitative reaction to the saccharine polyester conformity of '70s **DISCO**, punk rock spawned several broad musical genres – themselves reactions to punk's perceived excesses – that would go on to form the basis of 1980s alternative and later mainstream culture, such as post-punk (including **GOTH**) and **NEW WAVE**. These "post-punk" movements themselves inspired a **HARDCORE** backlash. Punk fashion, with its striking originality, accessibility, aggression, deliberately transgressive aspects and powerful visual impact was rapidly assimilated not only by musicians from other genres but also by popular fashion – selectively and usually in a toned-down configuration. By the end of the 1980s, cyberpunk – an alloy of punk philosophy and aesthetics with more traditional post-war and 1960s–70s "new wave" science fiction tropes – was firmly established and set to grow in the following decade as the rise of the Internet in the '90s brought many of its uneasy dreams to life. *"Society made me what I am." "That's bullshit. You're a white suburban punk, just like me." (From "Repo Man," 1984.)*

put the move on *phrase* To make romantic advances to someone, particularly in an unwelcome or clumsy fashion. Also, by extension, to try to cajole someone into doing anything. *"Ben looks pretty decent in denim, too. I think you should put the move on this guy." (From "Magnificent Lover" by Karen Whittenburg, 1986.)*

queer *adjective* Gay. While this term was reclaimed in a positive, inclusive sense in the very late 1980s and early '90s, in the '80s it was still primarily used with a variably negative and insulting intention. This usage goes back to the early years of the twentieth century and possibly before, based on the word's standard English meaning (descriptive of an unusual, puzzling, or eccentric person or thing). Secondly, the term was commonly used to pejoratively imply unmanly traits or behavior. Also used as a noun, in both senses. In the citation the term is employed strictly in the first sense and not the second, the speaker jumping to the sincere but mistaken conclusion that he finds himself on the receiving end of an impolite proposition. *"You wanna make ten bucks?" "Fuck you, queer." "Now wait a minute, wait a minute, kid, you got the wrong idea. [...] I can't leave [my wife's] car in this bad area." (From "Repo Man," 1984.)*

rack up *verb* To steal, particularly to shoplift, and especially to thieve supplies related to graffiti. The practitioners of this discipline traditionally consider it beneath their dignity as artists to pay for materials that will be used not for mere personal gain but for the public-spirited beautification of the community. *"One of the most common methods of racking up paint is to hide it in the sleeves or down the front of a large ski parka or fatigue jacket." (From "Getting Up: Subway Graffiti in New York" by Craig Castleman, 1982.)*

rad *adjective* Abbreviation of **RADICAL**. *"It's my new pool patio. Bitchin', huh?" "It's pretty rad." (From "Earth Girls are Easy," 1988.)*

radical *adjective* **AWESOME**, extreme, tremendous. Originally surfer slang, later mainstream. The term's origin (from the Latin radix, "root") provides its slang connotation: that something is considered to be so **COOL** because, far from being derivative, it goes back to fundamentals and provides a whole new outlook on or concept of the subject – as in "a radical departure." *"Hey, Bernie, what a radical party!" (From "Weekend at Bernie's," 1989.)*

rainmaker *noun* One who is particularly skilled at attracting new clients or customers, or otherwise persuading others into taking action beneficial to the business. Think Templeton "Faceman" Peck from "The A-Team." Derives from African and Native American history, both cultures separately developing rituals with the identical purpose of encouraging the rainfall necessary for their continued survival. *"This political rainmaker is also one of the shrewdest, most effective backroom operatives ever to put on a Senate toga." (From "Survival of the Fattest" by Larry Zolf, 1984.)*

Ralph *verb* To vomit, **BLOW CHUNKS**. Onomatopoeic term based on the whimsical notion that one vomiting might in fact be shouting that name. Often associated with the similarly derived "Huey" ("calling Huey and Ralph on the big white telephone," and many variations on that theme). *"Your middle name is Ralph, as in puke." (From "The Breakfast Club," 1985.)*

Rambo *noun* Epithet for a thoughtlessly gung-ho person, courageous to the point of imbecility, quick to resort to physical violence without adequately exploring alternatives; a glory hound. The enthusiastic Cadet Eugene Tackleberry from 1984's "Police Academy" and its sequels is a perfect example. As in the citation, the appellation is ripe for sarcastic application to any cowardly, conflict-averse, or sensibly cautious person. *"You can come out now, Rambo." (From "Weekend at Bernie's," 1989.)*

rancid *adjective* Unpleasant, foul, disgusting, ugly: substandard in any sense. Standard English made slang by hyperbolic usage. *"Joan shook her head, not sure if she was teasing Vicki or if she really wanted to pound on her for making it all sound so rancid." (From "A Certain Slant of Light" by Margaret Wander Bonanno, 1980.)*

rap *noun* A form of vocal musical performance characterized by rhythmically spoken lyrics delivered in a syncopated, rapid-fire manner. A key component of **HIP HOP**, rap music rose into mainstream popularity with the precipitous early 1980s fall from grace of **DISCO** (though rap itself and its antecedents greatly predate this popularity). Old-school rapping tended to be fairly simple, but later "golden age" (mid-1980s to early '90s) techniques became significantly more complex. "Rap" (verb) had long been slang for talking or speaking, from which the genre takes its name. Debate has long swirled over the title of "first true rap record," often claimed for The Sugarhill Gang's 1979 "Rapper's Delight," but the consensus is that it was preceded by "King Tim III (Personality Jock)" from The Fatback Band. In the latter half of the 1980s the tone of rap music changed significantly with the rise of **GANGSTA** rap, fueled by Ice-T and NWA's aggressive and explicit work. *(Ref. "I'm Bad" by LL Cool J, 1987.)*

raw *adjective* Excellent, **COOL** (skateboarding term, originally). *"Hey, drinks on the Bozeman." "Hey, all right, Boze, man, let's rock. This is raw!" (From "Thrashin'," 1986.)*

reach out and touch someone *phrase* To make a phone call. From AT&T's highly successful advertising slogan, used from 1979. As in the citation, often employed with sinister intent. *"The 'White Pages,' my favorite. You ever actually reach out and touch someone?" [Without waiting for reply, whacks adversary with phone book.] (From "Dragnet," 1987.)*

read my lips *phrase* Instruction to the listener that he or she should give full attention and regard to the words coming out of one's mouth. In popular use throughout the decade, but especially memorably employed by George HW Bush in his acceptance of the Republican nomination in 1988: "Read my lips: no new taxes."

reefdogger *noun* A marijuana cigarette; synonymous with and an elaboration upon "reefer."

relax *verb* See **CHILL**.

rents *noun* The **PARENTAL UNIT**s; those who pay the rent. *"As we learned last year, 'rents are 'parents,' with only the vestigial last syllable pronounced." (From "New York Times" magazine's "On Language" column, by William Safire, September 22, 1985.)*

rep *noun* Abbreviation of "reputation." An intangible but vitally important word-of-mouth record of character which must be protected and nurtured at all costs. Per Shakespeare's Othello, "Oh, I have lost my reputation! I have lost the immortal part of myself, and what remains is bestial." Also an instance of a physical exercise (abbreviation of "repetition"); for example, one correctly executed push-up is one rep. *"You can't just disappear in the middle of Kumite like that! I got a rep to uphold, you know?" (From "Bloodsport," 1988.)*

retard *noun* A foolish or uncoordinated person. See **TARD**. While the term clearly denotes intellectual disability, in practice it was used more as an accusation of thoughtlessness or clumsiness. The insult would never have been considered innocuous, but it would be far less likely to raise eyebrows in the 1980s than today as the term "mental retardation" was standard professional medical parlance at the time. *"You suck, you know that?" "Retard!" (From "National Lampoon's Vacation," 1983)*

retarded *adjective* Of a thing or activity: stupid, poorly planned, pointless. See **RETARD**.

richie *noun* A rich person or one from a rich family (see also **PREPPY**). Derives from the comic book character Richie Rich, "the poor little rich boy." *"He's so beautiful…. He's a richie." "Uh, a whattie?" "A richie. It's kind of stupid. It's just his family has a lot of money." (From "Pretty in Pink," 1986.)*

ridiculous *adjective* Amazing, unbelievable – in either a positive or negative sense. *(Ref. "Delirious" by ZZ Top, 1985.)*

righteous *adjective* Tremendous, extremely **COOL**. Applicable to anything, but particularly when used in reference to a person the term carries a bombastically amplified sense of its conventional meaning; virtuous, morally without stain or blemish, one who walks tall and conducts himself or herself with honor in this fallen world. *"Oh, he's very popular, Ed. The sportos, the motorheads, geeks, sluts, bloods, wastoids, dweebies, dickheads – they all adore him. They think he's a righteous dude." (From "Ferris Bueller's Day Off," 1986.)*

rip *verb* To do something in a confident, skillful, impressive fashion. Originally surfer slang. Also (verb or noun) a version of **RIP OFF**. *"Sequence rips, you're really shredding." "Yeah? Think so?" "Yeah, you really tore it up. I can get you in the magazines." (From "North Shore," 1987.)*

rip off *verb* To steal, defraud, or trick someone out of something. "Rip" has been used in prison slang since the early 1900s, from which "rip off" developed and emerged into mainstream usage, where it remains. "Rip-off" or "ripoff" as a noun, meaning a copy, forgery, or imitation – or even an outright robbery – also became popular in the 1960s and continues in mainstream usage today. *"You know your friends? […] They totaled the gas station, and then they ripped off my van!" (From "Earth Girls are Easy," 1988.)*

ripped *adjective* To have a very low body fat percentage, resulting in clearly defined muscles, veins, and muscle striations, particularly in reference to the abdominal muscles ("abs"). See also **CHISELED**. *(Ref. "Attack on the Stars," by Sir Mix-A-Lot, 1988.)*

roach *noun* The unsmokable butt of a marijuana cigarette, often including a tip of rolled paper or cardboard to avoid wastage, but always smoked down to finger-burning shortness (unless an alligator clip, pair of tweezers, or similar device – known as a "roach clip" – is used). The etymology of this usage is uncertain. It's tempting to suggest that "roach" is used because the discarded butts resemble the insects, but that tenuous connection would occur only to the severely chemically disadvantaged as, in contrast to cockroaches, marijuana joint butts are small, generally light in color and usually legless. Nonetheless, something more in the line of a cigar butt might be forgivably mistaken for a cockroach from a distance, so perhaps there is some connection. An entirely different possible origin is that "roach" (verb) also means to cut or clip something down to a smaller size; particularly a horse's mane (a "roached mane" resembles a flattop haircut). The "roached" joint has been similarly reduced in length. This definition, incidentally, means that "roach clip" is a tautology. Finally, in Spanish slang, "tabaco de cucaracha" ("roach tobacco") is low-quality tobacco powder, possibly so called due to its resemblance to cockroach feces. Either way, the term's use in English dates back at least to the jazz subculture of the late 1930s and probably earlier. *(Ref. "Cheeba Cheeba" by Tone-Loc, 1989.)*

roach coach *noun* A food truck or catering trailer of the type found at construction sites, movie location shoots, and so on. So named on account of such vehicles' perceived lack of hygiene and thus their numerous real or imagined free riders. *"That is the mobile food service affectionately called the 'roach coach,' or some other derogatory name." (From "Good Food for a Sober Life" by Jack Mumey and Anne S. Hatcher, 1987.)*

road pizza *noun* Flattened, more or less unidentifiable roadkill.

road rage *noun* Violent, emotional behavior experienced while driving, usually caused by other motorists' infractions of driving etiquette and resulting in negative effects ranging from public insult to intentional vehicle collisions and shooting fatalities. Though by no means an entirely new phenomenon (note the citation's date) several shootings on congested Los Angeles roads during the summer of 1987 caused widespread fear of what local media initially termed "highway hostility,"[1] though "road rage" won through as the preferred phrase and subsequently rocketed in popularity during the 1990s. See also the punning derivative **ROID RAGE**. *"All of a sudden, people are shooting each other on the freeways. Why? What's behind this new phenomenon, 'Road Rage'?" (From "To Love and Live Again," by David E. Ritzenhaler, 1984.)*

road warrior *noun* Desperately magniloquent term for a traveling salesman or executive. Derives from the movie "The Road Warrior" (1982), sequel to 1979's "Mad Max," in which a solitary, disturbed loner roams a bleak wasteland with little prospect of reward and no chance of mercy or redemption, accompanied only by his faithful dog. In contrast, real-world "road warriors" were rarely able to find pet-friendly accommodation. *"It could be the most important meeting of your year. And you were totally prepared.... Until you snagged your stockings. But being a Road Warrior, you're staying at Howard Johnson where they keep a Road*

---

1. "Highway Hostility Must Be Stopped: L.A. Needs a Return to Civility, Drastic Moves on Congestion" ("Los Angeles Times," August 23, 1987).

Warrior Emergency Kit at the front desk at all times." (Advertisement from "News-week" magazine, 1989.)

rock *verb* To be glorious. That which rocks is not merely **COOL** but also skillfully energetic or, of an object, divinely formed in the pursuit of a noble goal. Synonym of **RULE**, antonym of **SUCK**. See also **ROCKING, ROCK OUT**. *(Ref. "Rio Rocks" by Sigue Sigue Sputnik, 1988.)*

rocket science *noun* Idiomatic metaphor for anything extremely complex or obscure, difficult to learn or perform, and/or likely to result in disaster if botched. Almost exclusively used in the negative sense, in absurd contrast to whatever simple, easy, trivial thing is being discussed. Identical in this sense to **BRAIN SURGERY** (see also for usage example). Later these two idioms would become mixed to create the nonexistent specialty "rocket surgery," but that was a late 1990s evolution. *"Your Honor, the point is not rocket science. It is clearly established that trees attract lightning." (From "American Jurisprudence Proof of Facts, Third Series," 1988.)*

rocking *adjective* Someone/something who/that **ROCK**s. Also (inter-jection) an expression of eager approval synonymous with **AWESOME**. *"Hey gang, you're rolling with Rockin' Ricky Rialto, the voice of Kingston Falls, USA!" (From "Gremlins," 1984.)*

rock out *verb* To perform music with energy and ability, or to dance enthusiastically or frenetically to music. Mainly used in reference to rock music, but the term is applicable to any genre, with the obvious exception of those types of music for which no such enthusiasm is possible, like modern jazz. *(Ref. "Louie Louie" by The Pretenders, 1981.)*

roid rage *noun* Violent mood swings and (self-)destructive behavior attributed to use of anabolic ste**ROIDS** by bodybuilders and other athletes. Play on **ROAD RAGE**. *"Steroid users may become more aggressive and more violent, a phenomenon known as 'roid rage.'" (From "The World Book Health and Medical Annual 1990," 1989.)*

roids *noun* Abbreviation of "anabolic steroids," artificial androgens employed by **JOCK**s (particularly bodybuilders) to enhance perfor-mance and appearance. Used by professional athletes since the 1950s, in the 1980s roids became relatively commonplace among iron-pumpers. See also **ROID RAGE**. *"So what if your hair starts to fall out and your heart beats twice as fast as it should. Besides, what could be wrong with 'roids?" (From "Steroid Users Often Driven by Desire for Results" by Tom Zucco, St. Petersburg Times, May 29, 1984.)*

rolf *verb* Variant of **RALPH**.

oller *noun* Police, particularly those in a prowl car[1] on patrol. Proba-bly an abbreviation of "patrollers," the meaning strengthened by the fact that such vehicles tend to roll around slowly and quietly after dark in order to surprise the unwary transgressor. *"Shit!" "What?" "Roll-ers." "No." "Yup." "Shit!" (From "The Blues Brothers," 1980.)*

---

1. "Prowl car" may itself be a phonetic garbling or misheard imita-tion ("mondegreen") of "patrol car."

roll out *verb* To leave, get moving. Usually with some purpose, journey, or mission in mind. Also simply "roll." *"Autobots, transform and roll out!" (From "The Transformers: The Movie," 1986.)*

room temperature IQ *phrase* Descriptive of a person of very low intelligence. Room temperature is conventionally considered to be around a comfortable 68–72 degrees Fahrenheit, which would be considered "Extremely Low" on the Wechsler intelligence classification scale. *"Lurking at the bottom [...] is the possibility that the room temperature IQ that informs every groove of [Redd Kross album] 'Neurotica' may very well be the real thing." (From "Spin" magazine, July 1987.)*

rule *verb* To occupy a position of victorious supremacy, as of a nation's monarch. Antonym of **SUCK**. *(Ref. "Love Rules" by Don Henley, from the soundtrack of the movie "Fast Times at Ridgemont High," 1982.)*

rush *noun* An exciting, adrenaline-spiking thrill. The term derives from the sudden onset of a drug and is related to "head rush," a sudden drop in blood pressure experienced when rising from a sitting or lying position (orthostatic hypotension). Also a Canadian prog rock band popular in the 1980s, and for many years previously and since, who wrote songs with unusual time signatures about space and Ayn Rand. Rush retains its place in the public eye partly for their musicianship and originality, but mainly due to people still making wisecracks about the **GEEK**iness of the band's fans. See also **TAKE OFF**. *"Jackson, what're you doing?" "You want a rush? I'll give you a rush!" (From "Action Jackson," 1988.)*

same difference *phrase* Assertion that there is in fact little or no difference between two things presented as choices or alternatives, or at least that choosing one or the other will make little difference in the long run. The phrase appears paradoxical, or at least oxymoronic, but in fact as commonly used it is simply linguistically meaningless. "Difference" refers to a relation between two or more objects/concepts, so a single object cannot itself possess a difference, and therefore it is impossible to compare the "differences" of two objects. However, it is of course entirely reasonable to compare the difference relations within two sets of objects. For example, the words in the set "dog, dogs" and those in the set "cat, cats" share the same difference; that in each set the second word is the plural of the first. *"I'm sure they didn't forget your birthday. They just didn't remember it right away." "Same difference." (From "Sixteen Candles," 1984.)*

say what? *phrase* "What did you say?" Either in genuine ignorance or, with particular emphasis on the "what," in incredulity (often exaggerated). *"The ... The ratings." [...] "We're ... number one." [Pause while Yankovic's head slowly swivels round.] "Say what?" (From "UHF," 1989.)*

scam *verb* To gain something by means of deception, to con. As a noun, an instance of such fraud. Possibly originating from carny (carnival worker) slang, the term entered widespread use in the early 1980s thanks to news reports surrounding the FBI's late 1970s and early '80s "Abscam" sting operation (see **MONEY TALKS AND BULLSHIT WALKS**). Also used in the '80s to describe the act of attempting to pick up women, based on the pessimistic assumption that success would be necessarily contingent on the use of trickery (see also **GAME**). *"I didn't kill anybody, I swear! This whole thing's a setup, a scam, a frame job!" (From "Who Framed Roger Rabbit," 1988.)*

scamster *noun* One who operates or takes part in a **SCAM**; a conman or flimflam artist. The gravity of the term's reference to serious crime is diminished by its phonetic suggestions of "scamp" and "hamster." *"The scamster operates on the premise that the lure of millions [...] can induce even the shrewdest of business owners to part with modest thousands." (From "The Venture Magazine Complete Guide to Venture Capital" by Clinton Richardson, 1987.)*

scarf *verb* To eat a lot, rapidly. Derives from the neckwear past which the devoured material speeds to its digestive doom. Also "scarf out" – equivalent to **PIG OUT**. See also **BARF**. *"Yeah, you know, like, Cindy Boo lost ninety pounds and even, like, scarfed on ice cream." [...] "Like, 'scarf and barf.'" (From "Valley Girl," 1983.)*

scenester *noun* One who is part of, wishes to be part of, or wishes to be seen to be part of a "scene" – which in this sense refers to a subculture or social group, as in "the LA **GOTH** scene." Not intended as a compliment.

schmooze *verb* To obsequiously socialize, usually with a specific target and outcome in mind (see **NETWORK**). Also, in a more positive sense, simply to converse. Derives from the Yiddish "shmuesn," meaning "to chat," which itself has its roots in the Hebrew "shemuah" meaning "rumor" or "report." Also "shmooze."

schtup *verb* To fornicate, particularly in a casual or extemporaneous fashion. From the Yiddish for "push." *"If you saw him schtup a different woman every weekend, then people would see him as cold and deliberate." (From "Mass Media Issues" by George R. Rodman, 1989.)*

schweet *adjective* **"schwee-heet"** Very cool, lucky, or pleasantly sur-prising. Variant of "sweet."

scope out *verb* To observe or analyze something, particularly from a distance. *"That's the one, dude. Scope it out." (From "Sixteen Candles," 1984.)*

score *verb, interjection* To obtain, acquire, or achieve something desir-able. Particularly sex, though this was more of a 1970s usage. Also used as an exclamation ("Score!") to acknowledge such an achieve-ment. *"Let's score some beers." (From "Lucas," 1986.)*

scoshe *noun* See **SKOSH**.

scratch *verb* To move a vinyl record forward and backward under the needle, causing the recorded audio to play faster, slower, backwards, and more or less unintelligibly; used as a form of percussion. Scratching, also known as "scrubbing," is responsible for the charac-teristic "wucka wucka" sound prevalent in 1980s **HIP HOP** records and ubiquitous in '80s hip hop **WANNABE** records. *(Ref. "Radiotron" by Firefox, featured in the movie "Breakin' 2: Electric Boogaloo," 1984.)*

screw job *noun* A **SCAM**, con trick, or other deception or conspiracy in which someone is being set up to get the unhygienic end of the stick in one way or another ("get screwed"). *"I think this is nothing but a goddamn screw job. I think it's a shakedown." (From "Raising Arizona," 1987.)*

scumbag *noun* A reprehensible, despicable, worthless person. Specifically, one who earns such utter contempt by way of sleazy, degenerate behavior. "Scum" refers to a layer of variably solid matter that forms on top of a liquid exposed to the atmosphere or waste matter that remains after various industrial processes. The word's first recorded use as an insult appears in the Christopher Marlowe play "Tamburlaine the Great" (1587/8): "These are the cruel pirates of Argier / That damned train, the scum of Africa." While a "scumbag" might be used to contain the useless, unpleasant substance after skimming it from the liquid in any relevant scenario, such an item appears to have been used specifically in the refining of sugar as far back as 1812. A simmered concoction is poured into a coarse "scum-bag" for straining, which is then pressed under a board to eliminate the useful material into a storage vessel and retain the useless "scum" within the bag. Also "scumbucket." *"Listen, pal. Your client's a scumbag, you are a scumbag, and scumbags see the judge on Monday morning." (From "RoboCop," 1987.)*

scum-sucking *adjective* Repulsive, degenerate, prone to foul habits. Derogatory. *"Well, you slime-eating dogs, you scum-sucking pigs, you sons of a motherless goat." (From "Three Amigos," 1986.)*

scuzz *noun* Schmutz, dirt, unidentifiable but definitely disgusting material of the type found as a residue in infrequently visited locations such as the interior of vacuum cleaners and the area underneath refrigerators. Possibly an amalgamation of "scum" (see **SCUMBAG**) and "fuzz." By extension, a person exhibiting similar qualities and (adjective) "scuzzy" – a person or thing resembling or evoking scuzz. Also "scuz." *"I'd appreciate it if you wouldn't use my comb, either. It's so full of scuzz I can't use it." (From "Mystic Pizza," 1988.)*

scuzzbag *noun* A slightly less distasteful version of **SCUMBAG**. See **SCUZZ**. Also "scuzzball," "scuzzbucket."

seriously *adverb, interjection* **"CIrrus-ly"** Extremely, emphatically. Pronounced with a great deal of stress on the first syllable. Also used as an affirmative, to encourage one's interlocutor to carry on talking, or as a simple exclamation (also interrogatively). Not exclusively **VALSPEAK** but a linguistic marker thereof, particularly when used in a fashion conspicuously different from its standard meaning or with flagrant emphasis.

shack up *verb* To reside, particularly in a cohabitational sense and/or temporarily. See also **POSSLQ**.

shades *noun* Sunglasses. A necessary accessory for any **RIGHTEOUS DUDE**, acting as an unmistakable nonverbal signal that one is **COOL**. *(Ref. "The Future's So Bright, I Gotta Wear Shades," by Timbuk 3, 1986.)*

Fig. 11: Iconic Sunglasses of the 1980s

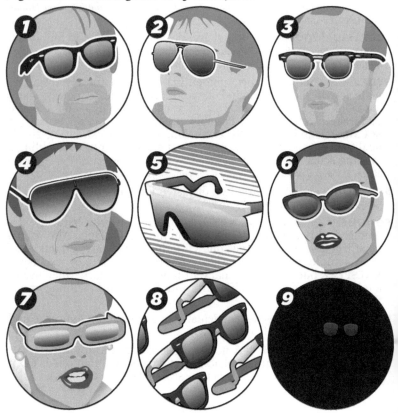

(1) Ray-Ban 4105 Wayfarers
(2) Ray-Ban 3025 Aviators
(3) Ray-Ban 3016 Clubmasters
(4) Linda Farrow 6031s
    and various similar Carerra Porsche Design models
(5) Oakley Razor Blades
    and other derivative single-lens sports/shield sunglasses
(6) Cat eye sunglasses
(7) Oversized plastic frame sunglasses
(8) Cheap, garish, two-tone neon Wayfarer knock-offs
    Croakies-brand retainer optional
(9) Sunglasses at night
    so you can, so you can, keep track of the visions in your eyes

shareware *noun* Computer software legally available without charge
the user being encouraged to redistribute the software (also free o
charge). Unlike **FREEWARE**, shareware was often monetized in som

form; for example, by having key features available only once a code (obtained by sending cash or a check to the developer via mail) had been entered. The "sharing" model was often chosen by smaller companies in order to avoid the **HASSLE**s of traditional mainstream distribution. *"The term 'shareware' describes a diverse collection of personal computer programs that range from one-file utilities to complete packages. [...] What they have in common is a unique approach to marketing." (From "Computerworld" magazine, May 1989.)*

shelled *adjective* To be badly, embarrassingly beaten. Originally used in baseball. This usage possibly derives from the obvious military sense but may (also) be a derivation of the older slang term "shellacked" (with identical meaning). *"So, a surprise move by Brown here, bringing in the Wild Thing, who's been shelled in two outings against the Yankees." (From "Major League," 1989.)*

shit happens *phrase* Existential observation remarking on the inevitability of negative events. Often used in reply to bad news, either in stoic commiseration or, in contrast, unsympathetically (see **FUCK THEM IF THEY CAN'T TAKE A JOKE**). A popular bumper sticker of the time. *"Kitten, I think what I'm saying is that sometimes shit happens, someone has to deal with it, and who you gonna call?" (From "Ghostbusters II," 1989.)*

shit-hot *adjective* Extremely capable or phenomenally talented. See also **HOT SHIT**. *"Koerner, Ray & Glover were the absolute shit-hot wildmen of the early '60s acoustic scene." (From "Spin" magazine, October 1988.)*

shitkicker *noun* City dweller's insult for a rural type, implying a lack of education, intelligence, skill, professionalism, or savoir faire. Also a popular taunt aimed at the "urban cowboy" type of the mid- to late 1970s, persisting into the '80s.[1] Originates from the fact that a farm worker or similar is more likely to encounter animal dung while going about his daily business than a city slicker. Also, there is the implication that only a completely harebrained bumpkin would, when chancing upon such a lump or pile of dung, entertain the thought that it might be one hell of a laugh to give it a good punt. *"This shitkicker couldn't strike me out with a hundred pitches." (From "The Natural," 1984.)*

shitload *noun* A large quantity of something, as in "truckload." Perhaps a corruption of the UK "shedload" (the amount that would fill an entire shed) or possibly simply the amount of a thing at which, being astonished by its remarkable abundance, one might reasonably exclaim, "Shit!" *"Listen, we're not just doing this for money.... We're doing it for a shitload of money!" (From "Spaceballs," 1987.)*

shitting bricks, shit a brick *phrase* Extremely nervous or terror-stricken, as would be expected of someone required to pass one or more large, rough, dry, pointy-edged objects ex recto. See also **DON'T HAVE A COW**. *"Rocky bit my thumb. [...] Him's nervous because Christmas is almost here." "Nervous or excited?" "Shitting bricks." "You shouldn't use that word." "Sorry. Shitting rocks." (From "National Lampoon's Christmas Vacation," 1989.)*

---

1. Satirized in The Vandals' 1982 track "Urban Struggle."

SHOCK JOCK

shock jock *noun* A radio personality of the type exemplified by Howard Stern (nationally syndicated since 1986), whose shows focus on entertaining the audience via aggressive, transgressive humor considered by some to be distasteful or objectionable. "Jock" in this sense derives from "disk jockey," itself originally a derisive term for one who would "ride" on the disks of others, not having the talent to produce music himself. *"Top Dallas shock-jock James 'Moby' Carney says: 'I pick on ladies. I pick on gays. I pick on fat white guys, rednecks and foreigners.'"* (From "US News & World Report," 1987.)

shred *verb* To perform outstandingly, with great energy, concentration, and phenomenal skill. Originally applied mainly to surfing but later and in more widespread usage to guitar playing, though this latter usage was prevalent more in the 1990s than '80s, brought into the mainstream by Pantera's "The Art of Shredding," from their major label debut album "Cowboys from Hell" (1990). *"Yeah, I hear he one hot ripper." "He one bad shredder, yeah? He bust his stick he shred so bad."* (From "North Shore," 1987.)

shrooms *noun* Hallucinogenic "magic" mushrooms; psilocybin. *"Hey, what, were you on shrooms or what?" (From "Hot Dog... The Movie," 1984.)*

sick *adjective* Something of mind-blowingly high quality, so extreme or of such intensity that it would nauseate or discombobulate a less experienced or hip person. An example of amelioration (see **BAD**). Simultaneously the term was commonly used in its standard form to refer to mental illness or bad taste, as in "you're sick," or "a sick joke." *"That [car] belongs to the slumlord that owns this place. It's his pride and joy." "It's pretty sick." (From "Some Kind of Wonderful," 1987.)*

sick building syndrome *phrase* Diagnosis of a workplace or other building in which design flaws, poor materials, lousy construction, or unsatisfactory maintenance allow or encourage the spread of disease (for example, by enabling the spread of mold spores). Also, more subtly, a workplace in which adverse effects such as employee sickness, stultification, or other loss of productivity are caused psychologically by negative environmental factors that impair the free flow of mental and physical activity. These factors may include overcrowding, lack of natural light or ventilation, flickering fluorescent tubes, obnoxious wallpaper, clam-brained co-workers etc. *"The video is most suitable for clients and building managers, alerting them to the reality of sick-building syndrome." (From "The Architect's Journal," 1989.)*

sike *misspelling* See **PSYCH**.

ska *noun* Music of Jamaican origin with its roots in the 1950s–60s characterized by a forceful offbeat rhythm rendering it danceable by those of even minimal musical or athletic ability. "2-Tone" ska began in the UK in the late 1970s, gaining some chart popularity in the early '80s with bands like The Specials and Madness. In the US, mainstream visibility was not so rapidly realized, with small Los Angeles and New York ska scenes built around the **NEW WAVE/PUNK** audiences and taking until the late '80s to break out and thereafter achieve chart prominence throughout the '90s.

skank *noun* In continuous usage since at least the 1930s to refer to an unhygienic female. See also **SKANKY**. Also (verb) to dance to **SKA** music, reggae, etc.

skanky *adjective* Repellent, nauseating, unhygienic. **VALSPEAK** but also in general usage. See also **SKANK**. *"A section [of the city] fraught with skanky third rate criminals, filth, and misfortune." (From "Spin" magazine, February 1989.)*

skate *verb* To ice-skate or skateboard and, by extension, to leave swiftly or to escape without punishment. As a noun, a task or mission requiring little effort. *"We'll get the Penguin's tax money. [...] Everything's gonna be all right. Let's skate." (From "The Blues Brothers," 1980.)*

skeezer *noun* A woman of easy virtue; a **SKEEZY** or disgusting person (also "skeevy," "skeevie"). *"Clarisse? You honked off with that skeezer?" (From "Lean on Me," 1989.)*

skeezy *adjective* Depressingly unpleasant due to the effects of poor hygiene and long-term bad habits. Possibly a blend of "sketchy" or **SKANKY** and "sleazy" (See **SLEAZE**). *(Ref. "Hoedown" by Special Ed, 1989.)*

skosh *noun* A small amount, smidgen. Derives from the Japanese "sukoshi," meaning "a little bit." Also "scoshe," "scosche," "scoche," "skoosh," etc. *"They're putting up the sign! How fun! ... It's a skosh crooked." (From "Mannequin," 1987.)*

slamdance *verb* To dance vigorously and violently at a **PUNK**, **HARDCORE**, thrash, etc. concert or club. Also "slamming." Described by the "New York Times" in 1981 as "the latest mode of dancing among the punks – sudden, full-tilt lunging across the floor that sometimes knocks other dancers off their feet." Used as a plot device in the notoriously cheesy "Next Stop, Nowhere" episode of "Quincy, ME" (1982) with the result that fake or unconvincing punks (see **POSER**) became known as "Quincy punks." See also **MOSH**. *"Watch me. You're gonna see some real slam-dancing." (From the "Quincy, ME" episode "Next Stop, Nowhere," 1982.)*

sleaze *noun* A sneaky, underhand, unpleasant, debauched person not to be trusted. Also "sleazebag," "sleazoid," etc. *"Hey, you sleaze! My bed!" (From "The Blues Brothers," 1980.)*

slime *noun* An unpleasant, viscous, sticky substance of no value and consequently an individual exhibiting similarly protoplasmic qualities. Also an unpleasant, viscous, sticky toy introduced by Mattell in 1976 and popular in the '80s. Both as a substance and as an insult, slime was a common component of 1980s movies and television. Use of the stuff was particularly prevalent in children's fantasy movies and messy game shows like Nickelodeon's "You Can't Do That on Television," largely as a result of the massive and enduring popularity of the muculent "Ghostbusters" (1984) character Slimer. Also, as a verb, to cover someone in slime ("He slimed me!") *"If all they were after was revenge against Jerry Caesar, I'd chalk it up to slime versus slime." (From "Dragnet," 1987.)*

Sloane Ranger *noun* UK slang for an urban (Sloane Square in London's Chelsea district, specifically) moneyed person either with rural affectations or with actual country estates. Think **PREPPY** but equipped with Barbour jackets and Range Rovers (making the term a double pun on the Lone Ranger). Often shortened to "Sloane." Diana, Princess of Wales was considered the epitome of the type and in 1982's "The Official Sloane Ranger Handbook" (a British reaction to the success of 1980's "The Official Preppy Handbook") was invested with the title "the 1980s Super-Sloane."

smooth move, ex-lax *phrase* Sarcastic statement in response to another's thick-witted utter failure, thoughtless faux pas, crass behavior, or monumental fuckup. The term "ex-lax" (sic; the brand-name is not capitalized) refers to anti-constipation medication responsible for many a smooth bowel movement and is therefore employed as the exemplar or archetype of the smooth operator in the same way that Sherlock Holmes is invoked to imply tremendous talent in detection (see **NO SHIT, SHERLOCK**). See also **NICE PLAY, SHAKESPEARE**.

snarf *verb* Originally to snatch greedily or to acquire in a sneaky way. By the 1980s the meaning had evolved: to eat in a ravenous, careless, frenzied fashion reminiscent of a fireman frantically shoveling coal into the firebox of a steam train pursued by bandits. Possibly simply onomatopoeic, possibly a blend of "snort" and **SCARF**. *"I still think Courtney snarfed those candy bars herself." (From "Who Framed Mary Bubnik?" – "Bad News Ballet" series #4 – by Jahnna N. Malcolm, 1989)*

so [...] *adverb* Declaration that something is passe, old-fashioned or obsolete, usefully specifying a year in which it would have been current, fashionable, or state of the art: "Oh, Jessica, come on; leg warmers are sooooo 1983."

solid *adjective* Approving agreement; "very good" in general. *"I got no beef with you, Flyguy. But I want Mr. Big." "Solid." (From "I'm Gonna Git You Sucka," 1988.)*

so sure *phrase* see **I'M SO SURE**.

soul patch *noun* A form of facial hair consisting of a small, squarish area of beard clinging apologetically to the labiomental groove between the lower lip and the chin. A favorite of jazz musicians. *"Ace had become a local sensation last fall when, in mid-season, he quit football rather than shave his soul patch." (From "National Lampoon" magazine, 1987.)*

sound bite *noun* In news reporting, politics, and marketing, a small segment extracted from a larger speech, article, etc., chosen for its simplicity and memorability and publicized with heavy repetition with the intention of having it stick indelibly in the memory. The term is often used in a pejorative sense to imply overly simplistic presentation of issues and/or cynical manipulation of an audience (particularly when the technique is employed by a **SPIN DOCTOR**) *"He is neither the first to master the basic rhythms of news coverage nor the only current retailer of sound-bite outrage." (From "New York" magazine, March 1988.*

sounds *noun* Music on radio, vinyl, cassette **TAPE**, etc. In use since the mid-1950s. *(Ref. "Radio Land," by Michael Martin Murphey, 1983.)*

space cadet *noun* Someone who is habitually "spaced out," possessing only a tenuous connection to mundane reality. Possibly a drug user, but by no means necessarily. *"Don't he think we could've got some other space cadet to hit Rebenga cheaper, too?" (From "Scarface," 1983.)*

spaz *noun* Derives from "spastic": a derogatory allusion to the movement disorder spastic diplegic cerebral palsy. In the US the word has been used fairly innocuously since the 1960s to refer to a clumsy person or, as a verb ("spaz out"), to refer to hyperactive behavior (similarly to **FREAK OUT**). In the UK, however, the term was widely employed in its original sense as a schoolyard insult in the 1980s and is now considered extremely cruel and unacceptable in polite society.

spiffy *adjective* New, high-quality, impressive, high-class, well-made, dapper, of neat appearance. Very old slang term, originally British, a derivative of "spiffing" (excellent), popular in the 1870s. *"Hi, Tommy. How you doing, man? [Indicates formal prom outfit.] Mighty spiffy." (From "Valley Girl," 1983.)*

spin doctor *noun* Particularly in politics, a person tasked with or highly skilled at the manipulation of public perception via media by putting a beneficial "spin" on potentially detrimental events. This activity is known as "spin control." A talented spin doctor can extract a positive from any negative by refocusing, reframing,[1] or entirely rewriting the narrative. The term, first notably used in a 1984 New York Times editorial discussing the Reagan/Mondale debates, is rarely intended as a compliment. "Spin" in this sense refers to the practice of imparting lateral or vertical angular momentum to a cue ball in billiards, pool, or snooker, causing it to behave in a desired manner when striking the object ball or a rail. Donald Regan, Ronald Reagan's confusingly-named White House Chief of Staff ('85–'87), was known as the "Director of Spin Control." See also **SOUND BITE**. *"A good spin doctor can take any set of facts and figures and turn them to the advantage of his candidate." (From "1989 NCAA Convention Proceedings," National Collegiate Athletic Association, 1989.)*

sport *verb* To possess or wear something ostentatiously. Very old English usage (18th century). *"Oh, my goodness. I am sporting a tremendous woody right now." (From "Short Circuit," 1986.)*

sport-ute *noun* Abbreviation of "sport utility vehicle." A type of automobile that would in later decades morph into something that was neither sporty nor particularly useful, but which in the 1980s was in its lean, youthful prime. Examples include the Ford Bronco and Suzuki Samurai, and of course the Jeep YJ (Wrangler), released in 1986 in response to consumer demand for a more well-mannered but still highly off-road capable all-round fun machine. Aficionados of

---

1. See **MIND FRAME**; the same metaphor applies, with the difference that the spin doctor shrinks or moves the frame of public attention with the deliberate intention of obscuring unwelcome facts.

the older, less refined CJ ("Civilian Jeep") contended that "YJ" stood for "**YUPPIE** Jeep." *"Reshaping the basic clay of your box-stock sport/ute is going to entail some expense." (From "Popular Mechanics" magazine, March 1988.)*

sprung *adjective* To be romantically infatuated with a person. *(Ref. "Beepers" by Sir Mix-A-Lot, 1989.[1])*

squid *noun* An unpleasant, limp, pale, rubbery, damp, gooey person; a **GRIMBO**. Also (mildly derogatory) a member of the US Navy. *"The strongest competition to 'squid' and 'grimbo' as successor term to 'nerd' is 'dexter,' a shortening of 'poindexter,' probably based on a cartoon character." (From "New York Times" magazine's "On Language" column, by William Safire, September 22, 1985.)*

squooshy *adjective* Pleasantly soft and crushable, comfortable; like "squishy" but without the implication of dampness. *"In the language of pillow advertising, squooshy has just been superseded by huggable. [...] Squooshy had a good run." (From "On Language; Miss Word of 1982" by William Safire, "New York Times" magazine, June 27, 1982.)*

Stella *noun* A mildly insulting term for an attractive young woman, with connotations of **AIRHEAD**edness, **DITZ**iness (see also **BOW-HEAD**), **VAL**leyism, and poor taste in music (see **DISCO**). *(Ref. "Blondie" by The Time, 1990.)*

stellar *adjective* Of a very high standard. *"It's a stellar jukebox, sir." "Thanks, Lloyd." (From "Say Anything...," 1989.)*

step off *verb* Injunction to back off, get out of one's face. *"Hey, what you doing, man? Step off! Step off! ... Did you bring any candy?" (From "The A-Team" episode "Mexican Slayride," 1983.)*

stoked *adjective* Excited, enthusiastic, and hopeful. Californian surfer/skater slang, originally. *"I could be wrong, but I think these ladies are stoked for us, Wyatt." (From "Weird Science," 1985.)*

stonewashed *adjective* Of denim, to have been artificially aged by being placed in a large rotating drum (such as that of an industrial washing machine) with sizable pumice stones. See also **ACID-WASHED, DESIGNER JEANS**. *"[Gain] confidence. Our street-style stone-washed karate Chi Vest, denim only. $36.95." (Mail order advertisement from "Black Belt" magazine, January 1986.)*

straight up *adverb* Directly, honestly. Also used as an intensifier. "You straight up nailed it!" *"Okay, straight up. I have a little group, and I think you'd fit in real well." (From "Purple Rain," 1984.)*

streetwise *adjective* In possession of the survival skills, toughness, and cynicism necessary for survival on the streets, particularly in the context of hardship, gang membership, hustling, or simply living in high-crime areas. Also abbreviated to "street" and used identically. "Vanilla Ice is street, man."

---

1. Béla Károlyi, cited in "Beepers" as an exemplar of girl-hugging, is the Hungarian and later American gymnastics coach particularly famed for consoling the American team after a controversial loss at the 1988 Olympics.

stressball *noun* Originally (1988) the trade name of an adult anxiety toy in the form of a soft polyurethane foam ball that, thanks to internal battery-operated microchip technology, emitted the sound of smashing glass on sensing an impact. The idea was that one could relieve work-related stress by throwing the ball and hearing the satisfying sounds of destruction without actually damaging anything (much). Later, the trademark – a minor victim of genericide – came to mean any squeezable ball intended to relieve stress through the action of repetitive gripping. *"Some shrinks claim Stress-ball is great as a form of play therapy." (From "Weekly World News" magazine, July 1989.)*

stud *noun* A masculine, sexually adept male. Since the early 19th century the word has referred to a stallion kept primarily for breeding purposes, and the term is used in much the same sense here. This usage, though highly popular in the 1980s, dates back to the late 19th century. *"Maverick, you big stud, take me to bed or lose me forever." (From "Top Gun," 1986.)*

stupid *adverb* Extremely or intensely. Also, as "get stupid" to party or **ROCK OUT**. *(Ref. "The Showstopper" by Salt-N-Pepa, 1986.)*

suck *verb* Of an event: to be unfortunate, negative, or unsatisfactory. Of a person: to be useless, contemptible, or malign. Of a place: to be run-down, inhospitable, or inadequate. Commonly believed to originate from the act of fellatio, though the concept of inferiority and inadequacy is conveyed more appropriately via the early 20th century idiom "suck the hind tit," itself based on the older saw "the runt pig always sucks the hind teat" (gets the least nourishing food source). Antonym of **RULE**. *"You think I'd join this crummy snobatorium? Why, this whole place sucks. That's right, it sucks." (From "Caddyshack," 1980.)*

sucka MC *noun* An incompetent or subpar rapper; one whose lack of originality results in tired repetition of clichéd tropes and **RIP-OFF**s of other artists' material. See **BITE**, **BITER**. *(Ref. "The Sounds of Science" by Beastie Boys, 1989.)*

sucker *noun* One who is naive, unwary, or not **STREETWISE** and thus easily **FOOL**ed; a mark, a simpleton. Used in the sense of an unweaned young animal (see **SUCK**). Often used in media of the 1980s as a family-friendly alternative to stronger profanity. Also "sucka," and internationally popularized in this form by Bosco Albert "BA" Baracus of The A-Team. *"What you doin', sucka? [...] This road leads directly to the airport, Hannibal." (From "The A-Team" episode "Mexican Slayride," 1983.)*

suck face *verb* To French kiss, particularly for an extended period or remarkably ravenously. See also **SWAP SPIT**. *"Hi. Want to dance, or would you rather just suck face?" (From "On Golden Pond," 1981.)*

sucky *adjective* Trash, useless, suboptimal. That which **SUCK**s. *"Yeah, well, yours are sucky white skates, like a figure skater, eh?" (From "The Adventures of Bob & Doug McKenzie: Strange Brew," 1983.)*

sup *abbr. phrase* Greeting; abbreviation of "What's up?" Usually employed in a slack, listless way apparently in expectation that the answer will be that nothing, or at least nothing of interest, is up.

sure as shit *phrase* Definitely, without a doubt. Also "shit-sure." *"The little booger's up to something, sure as shit." (From "Porky's II: The Next Day," 1983.)*

surf nazi *noun* In a positive sense, an obsessive surfer who employs rigorous, zealous discipline. In a quite distinct and negative sense, a surfer or group of surfers who protect "their" territory in an aggressive and usually illegal "locals only" manner. *"M: Do you think that [...] you might walk away from [surfing] again a few years down the line? K: No. Like I said, I'm a surf nazi now." (From "Surfer" magazine, 1988.)*

swap spit *phrase* To tongue kiss; used in a mildly derisory sense. See also **SUCK FACE**.

sweet *adjective* See **SCHWEET**.

swirly *noun* Form of bullying or retributive humiliation. For aggressors or seekers of justice, depending on perspective, to invert the victim base over apex, place his head in a toilet bowl, and flush. "Swirl" refers to the vortex of draining water. Requires teamwork; one person is usually insufficient, more than three are unlikely to fit in the cubicle. A convincing argument in favor of homeschooling. See also **MELVIN**.

tag *verb* To inscribe one's signature (itself also – noun – known as a "tag") on a wall or other piece of public or private property as a way of gaining fame or marking territory. *"It's a matter of getting a tag on each line, in each division, ya know, it's called 'going all-city.'" (From "Style Wars," 1983.)*

take a chill pill *phrase* See **CHILL PILL**.

take off *interjection* **"take off, eh"** Go away, get lost, figuratively or literally. Canadian dialect popularized by Bob and Doug McKenzie (see **HOSER**). Truncation of "take off to the Great White North," a reference to the snowy Canadian wilderness. Also the title of the McKenzies' breakout hit single, featuring Geddy Lee of the band **RUSH**, which reached #16 on the US Billboard Hot 100 singles chart. *(Ref. "Take Off" by Bob & Doug McKenzie, 1981.)*

tape *noun* Formally known as a "Compact Cassette" or, when containing pre-recorded audio, a "Musicassette," the cassette tape was the preeminent medium for the consumption of recorded music in the early to mid-1980s and precursor to the **CD**. It was also used by several popular 8-bit home computers (see **COMMODORE**) for data storage prior to large-scale adoption of the **FLOPPY** disk. A plastic clam-shell box containing a large quantity of magnetic tape (approximately 9½ feet of tape per minute of audio) wound onto two connected spools, the cassette would be placed inside a cassette recorder/player, whose geared drive wheels mesh with the teeth of the cassette's reels and, when rotating, cause the magnetic tape to be pulled from one spool, pass across an electromagnetic record/playback head, and be wound onto the other spool. The magnetic tape contains four separate tracks of recorded audio (two sets of left and right stereo tracks) and the cassettes are therefore reversible, having an A-side and B-side, with the tape in the correct position to start playing the B-side at the A-side's conclusion. A sixty-minute cassette thus consists of two thirty-minute sides. While tapes were useful for the large-scale distribution of pre-recorded music, their truly revolutionary application was their capacity to record music from the radio and to duplicate music from other tapes, vinyl records, etc. This facility caused much agitation among music industry executives.[1] Consequently, producing home-recorded tapes

---

1. The Dead Kennedys' "In God We Trust, Inc." cassette tape release contained all the songs on the A-side, with the B-side left blank and marked "Home taping is killing record industry profits! We left this side blank so you can help."

as gifts was not only a thoughtful favor to the recipient but also a mildly thrilling, subversive act of micropiracy. See also **BOOMBOX, BOOTLEG, MIX TAPE.**

Fig. 12: Cassette Tape & Dual Deck Mix Tape Creation

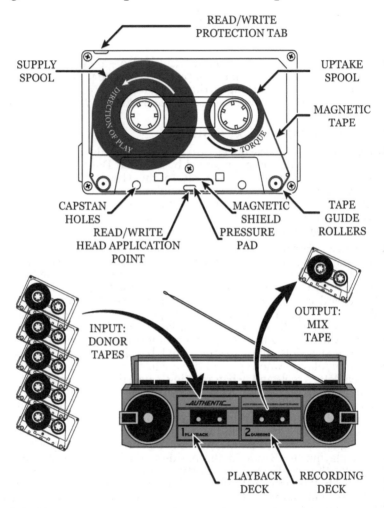

READ/WRITE
PROTECTION TAB

SUPPLY
SPOOL

UPTAKE
SPOOL

MAGNETIC
TAPE

DIRECTION OF PLAY

TORQUE

CAPSTAN
HOLES

READ/WRITE
HEAD APPLICATION
POINT

MAGNETIC
SHIELD
PRESSURE
PAD

TAPE
GUIDE
ROLLERS

INPUT:
DONOR
TAPES

OUTPUT:
MIX
TAPE

AUTHENTIC

1 PLAYBACK   2 DUBBING

PLAYBACK
DECK

RECORDING
DECK

tard *noun* A foolish or uncoordinated person. Abbreviation or **RETARD**: one who is "retarded" or literally "held back" in the sense of being inhibited from learning by a developmental disability. Today considered highly insensitive and objectionable but at the time generally used in a manner roughly equivalent to **DIPSHIT**.

ta-tas *noun* The female breasts, particularly those of the jaunty, alert type.

Technicolor yawn *noun* Poetic metaphor for the result of vomiting, particularly after overindulgence in alcohol, inspired by the ability of both emesis and the eponymous motion picture process to deliver startlingly hyperrealistic chromatic vividity. *(Ref. "So Fucked Up" by Sloppy Seconds, 1987.)*

technopreneur *noun* An entrepreneur in the field of technology. Something of a new phenomenon in the 1980s, as prior to the personal computer revolution and its famed garage-based startups (Apple, Microsoft, etc.) technological change was traditionally the preserve of large public companies like IBM and Hewlett-Packard. *"This book is Mr. Sculley's own telling of his transition from sugar-water salesman to technopreneur." (From "The Economist" magazine, 1987.)*

thang *noun* See AIN'T NO THANG.

that's the ticket *phrase* See YEAH, THAT'S THE TICKET.

thick *adjective* Appreciative term for a well-built, curvaceous female. *(Ref. "Freaky Tales" by Too Short, 1987.)*

thongs *noun* Beach sandals of the type now generally known as "flip-flops." *"He got lucky, and they now live on Maui. [...] I hope he trips on his thongs and falls into a volcano." (From "The Golden Girls" episode "The Engagement," 1985.)*

thrash *noun* Variant of HEAVY METAL emphasizing volume, speed, precision, and aggression. Also (verb, surfing) to SHRED.

tight *adjective* Something COOL or of high quality, with connotations of precision and skill from the conventional sense (e.g., "flying in tight formation"). *(Ref. "U Can't Touch This" by MC Hammer, 1990.)*

tits *adjective* Used adjectivally, excellent, outstandingly good. "That's tits!"

T n' A *abbr. phrase* Non-pornographic but intentionally titillating images of the female form, employed in media to attract male attention: "tits and ass."

toast *noun* One who is toast is finished, done, history, yesterday's news. Usage in this sense originates from an ad-lib by Bill Murray on the set of "Ghostbusters" (see citation; the original line in the shooting script reads "I'm gonna turn this guy into toast"). He who hesitates is toast. *"All right, this chick is TOAST." (From "Ghostbusters," 1984.)*

to die for *phrase* Something so spectacular its acquisition would be worth putting one's life on the line. A good example of the hyperbole for effect common throughout 1980s teen Californian slang. *"Wait 'til you see this new dress Cindy bought! I swear, it is to die for!" (From "Can't Buy Me Love," 1987.)*

toss one's cookies *phrase* To lose one's lunch, vomit. See BARF, BLOW CHUNKS, RALPH, TECHNICOLOR YAWN. *"Tossing your cookies.... Oh, that's more slang!" (From "Twins," 1988.)*

totally *adverb, interjection* Exclamation of complete agreement when used alone and, when used of an adjective, an extreme intensifier ("That's **TOTALLY AWESOME**"). Often used for effect when no intensity is required or indeed even possible ("She totally walked out, dude"). Californian, **VAL**-ish but geographically widespread and very popular. *"You could be coming out to California with me." [affects Californian accent] "Yeah, right! I'd get a totally bitchin' education out there, dude.... California." (From "The Sure Thing," 1985.)*

totally awesome *adjective* Of exceptionally impressive quality. See **AWESOME**. *"Fuckin' A, man, that jump was totally awesome." (From "Hot Dog... The Movie," 1984.)*

totally out *adjective* Completely unfashionable or unacceptable. See **OUT**.

totally tubular *adjective* Manifestly and undeniably **TUBULAR**. One of those expressions that was so overused by those trying to appear **COOL** (as in the citation) that it was already mainly used satirically by the end of the decade. *"This stuff is totally tubular, OK? [...] She's lighting it here. Is this cool or what?" (From "Club Paradise," 1986.)*

to the curb *phrase* Something of no consequence or of bad quality, to be regarded and treated as trash – deposited at the side of the road for pickup. Also "kick to the curb." *(Ref. "Radio Suckers" by Ice-T, 1988.)*

to the max *phrase* Extremely; to the ultimate possible level. Of Californian origin. *(Ref. "Shocked and Grossed" by the Mentors, 1985.)*

tough love *noun* Technique for correcting destructive or negative behavior, particularly but not exclusively employed by parents of rebellious teenagers, by means of actions that disregard the feelings of the person in question in favor of harsh and sometimes drastic measures. The approach emerged in the late 1960s and became very popular in the 1980s with the rise of the "troubled teen" industry. Of debatable effectiveness. *"For many years I practiced generic tough love. The emphasis was on the tough, not on the love." (From "Recovery from Rescuing" by Jaqueline Castine, 1989.)*

tough shit *interjection* Expression indicating a lack of sympathy. Emphatic modification of the much older expression "tough titty." See also **SHIT HAPPENS**. *"Vincent, get in the car, this is embarrassing." [...] "Tough shit!" (From "The Color of Money," 1986.)*

trash *verb* To ransack or destroy something. *"Tonight, those bastards, they trashed our house." (From "Revenge of the Nerds," 1984.)*

trash talk *noun* To verbally insult an opponent, particularly in sport with the object of taking his or her mind off the game. Best accomplished by means of creative, visceral language that creates strong colorful mental images that are difficult for the target to ignore. Frowned upon in many sports, but near-mandatory in others. *"With the proper practice, you should perform 60 percent better than you might have with trash talk in your mind." (From "Black Belt" magazine, June 1989.)*

trendie *noun* A dedicated follower of orthodox fashion and popular culture. A term of derision employed by dedicated followers of heterodox fashion and unpopular culture. Carries implications of naivety, vapidity, and an absence of critical thinking.

trendoid *noun* One who robotically follows fashion; a mixture of **TRENDIE** and "android." *"A trust-fund trendoid named Guy."* (From "New York" magazine, May 1986.)

trés *adverb* Very. Directly from the French. **VALSPEAK**, or at least affectedly aspirational (or satirizing such types, as in the cited lyrics). (Ref. "Les Nouveaux Riches" by 10cc, 1981.)

trip *verb* To be under the effect of a hallucinatory drug and thus out of touch with the real world. Consequently used to express extreme, delirious enjoyment of something. Also as an accusatory term ("You're tripping!") used of someone whose speech or other behavior is so bizarre or irrational as to be explicable only by such drug use. (Ref. "I Ain't Trippin'" by Too Short, 1988.)

tripendicular *adjective* Surpassingly, deliriously enjoyable or excellent. Surfer and later **VAL**ley slang with scantly documented etymology, though presumably based on "perpendicular." The "tri" prefix denotes the number three, and "pendicular" comes from the Latin "pendiculum" meaning "plumb line" (itself deriving from "pendere" meaning "to hang") and refers to a line intersecting another line at ninety degrees, as a plumb line hangs relative to the earth's surface. Thus, "tripendicular" might conceivably be claimed to mean "to be at a ninety-degree angle to all three dimensions simultaneously." Considering that each of the three conventional dimensions is already perpendicular to the other two, we find an apparent paradox: a line perpendicular to one dimension must therefore be parallel with another and so cannot be simultaneously perpendicular to it. Therefore, this interpretation may be a fair description of the bewildered, non-Euclidean state of mind of anyone who voluntarily uses this hyperbolic, elliptical word.

troop *verb* To walk, particularly for a long distance or, in **HIP HOP** parlance, in large numbers with the intent to project a powerful image or employ numerical superiority in a disagreement. *(Ref. "Strictly Snappin' Necks" by EPMD, 1989.)*

tubular *adjective* Perfect, extremely good, breathtaking. Derives from surfing jargon, in which activity a tube-like wave barrel – hollow, curved, clearly defined – is the ideal. The term spread thence to the **VALLEY GIRLs** who emulated the surf subculture. See also **TOTALLY TUBULAR**. *"Everybody thinks Tommy is so tubular and all, you know?"* (From "Valley Girl," 1983.)

tude *noun* See **BAD ATTITUDE**.

tuneage *noun* Any form of music; that which belongs to the class "tunes." Example of the **-AGE** suffix. Also "tunage," despite the fishy spelling. *"Their best release to date. The tuneage rocks more heavily than previous releases."* (From "Maximum Rocknroll" Issue #73, July 1989.)

twitchin' *adjective* Family-friendly variant of **BITCHIN'**.

unglitzy *noun* Down-to-earth, plain, straightforward. Generally used in a positive, complimentary sense, implying that lavish, gaudy decoration (etc.) would be unnecessary or detrimental. *"Goldberg seeks out such unglitzy but entertaining outings for his 2,000 members." (From "Kiplinger's Personal Finance" magazine, December 1986.)*

UVs *noun* **"you-vees"** Ultraviolet rays of the type emitted by the sun which, penetrating the epidermis, cause melanocytes to produce melanin and thus a suntan. Despite the entirely passive nature of tanning, UVs are often presented as requiring active capture ("Hey, let's go catch some UVs,") perhaps in an attempt to liven up the pastime's lethargic image.

Val *adjective* Abbreviation of "Valley," referring to the San Fernando Valley, CA, and adjectivally applicable to any person, thing, or concept emanating from that geographic location. Usually not intended as a compliment. See also **VALLEY GIRL**, **VALSPEAK**. *"Beat it, you Val jerk." (From "Thrashin'," 1986.)*

Valley girl *noun* A species of young female endemic to the San Fernando Valley region of Los Angeles County, CA, particularly in the late 1970s and throughout the '80s and '90s. Typically originating in well-off families and with a peripheral interest in the nearby coastal surf culture, this cliquish type emerged into the cultural limelight due to its fascinatingly unique combination of ferocious materialism and outlandish dialect (see **VALSPEAK**). Further traits of the stereotype include a ruthless attitude to social distinctions and groupings, a preoccupation with a small number of rigidly defined activities (tanning, partying, and going to the Sherman Oaks Galleria or, failing which, an inferior mall) and a less than scholarly approach to intellectual accomplishment (see **AIRHEAD, BOW-HEAD, DITZ**). Already present in the wider public consciousness by the very early '80s, the subculture was given a tremendous boost in prominence by Frank Zappa's satirical 1982 hit single "Valley Girl" (featuring his fourteen-year-old daughter delivering a Valspeak monologue) and the 1983 movie "Valley Girl." By this time, the type's characteristics had been effectively cemented and the Valley girl was a firmly established trope in movie and TV. Though sharing some characteristics, the Valley girl is definitely not to be confused with the **PREPPY** type; consider the difference between hot pink LA Gear hi-tops on the one hand (foot) and well-worn brown Sperry Topsiders on the other. *"To Julie, his favorite Valley girl, Randy sends his undying love and says [adopts Californian accent] 'Like comeback soon yaknow.'" (From "Valley Girl," 1983.)*

Valleyite *noun* A denizen of the San Fernando VALley, CA.

Valspeak *noun* Sociolect of the **VALLEY GIRL** and others both within Southern California and elsewhere. Strongly influenced by surfers' jargon and manner of speech. Contains most of the aspects of 1980s slang most despised by parents and educators of the time as egregious abuses of the English language (see **AWESOME, LIKE, TOTALLY**). Tonally, Valspeak is primarily characterized by its use of the "high rising terminal," in which the end of each clause rises in tone? Making everything sound like a question? "Vocal fry," also known as "creaky voice," is another Valspeak trait. An exaggerated SoCal accent (whether native or adopted) is also a key component, combining variably nasal and occasionally squeaky enunciation with loose-jawed vowel distortions ("so" becomes "seew," "really" becomes "rilly," **COOL** becomes "queue-el," "normal" becomes "nermal," etc.) Valspeak is above all a performative art and thus demands exaggeration in every available dimension. Valspeak vocabulary also includes **AS IF, BAG YOUR FACE, BARF ME OUT, BITCHIN', FOR SURE, GAG ME** (also ~ **WITH A SPOON**), **GNARLY, GRODY** (also ~ **TO THE MAX**), **GROSS** (also ~ **ME OUT THE DOOR**), **I'M SO SURE, JOANIE, SERIOUSLY, TRÉS, TRIPENDICULAR, TUBULAR, WHATEVER, XLNT/ZLINT.** Due to California's enviable position as the media and entertainment hub of the world and therefore humankind's primary memetic generator, Valspeak was soon eagerly adopted nationally and internationally. Frank Zappa, responsible for the hit single "Valley Girl" (abetted by his daughter Moon) described this process as "cultural pollution."[1] Thankfully, interpersonal communication expert Dr. Lillian Glass promised that "The Phase 1 Valley Girl is still a member of your family. [...] Caught at this stage, her transformation might still be nipped in the bud, although any too-vigorous attempt to do so is liable to result in a **PUNK** or **NEW WAVE** mutation, the deprogramming of which is beyond the scope of any book."[2] *"Valspeak fits into [...] the syndrome of secret languages; and though speakers of this secret language aren't aware, Valspeak is as closely governed by rules as are the classical languages of Greek and Latin." (From "A Few Words" by Laurence F. McNamee and Kent Biffle, 1988.)*

vegetate *verb* See **VEG OUT**.

veg out *verb* To engage in passive, lazy inactivity such as watching television. Also "vegetate." Derives from the vegetable's famously complete absence of mental or physical activity. The cautionary implication is that the longer one spends in this state the more leguminous one will become (see **COUCH POTATO**). *"Maybe I should grab that bottle and veg out with you." (From "A Nightmare on Elm Street," 1984.)*

VHS *noun* "Video Home System." Popular home video format developed by JVC. Winner of the video format wars, defeating Sony's **BETAMAX** format. While technically inferior to its competitor, VHS offered significant usability benefits and lower cost that ensured its victory. This became a famous cautionary lesson in human-centered design – the sort of thing parents tell their kids about at night if they want them to grow up to be engineers. *"I'm gonna need a VHS copy of all this by Monday for my Princeton application." (From "Heathers," 1989.)*

video jockey *noun* A television host who appears in between music video segments. Emergent with the rise of MTV, the term derives from the radio "disc jockey" (see **SHOCK JOCK** for origin). Also "VJ." *"Everett was, in effect, the first-ever rock-video jockey, and he was a great one." (From "The Rolling Stone Book of Rock Video" by Michael Shore, 1984.)*

vogues *noun* Custom aftermarket wheels and tires, particularly alloy rims and whitewall tires. From the Vogue Tyre (sic) and Rubber Co., established 1914. *(Ref. "My Hooptie" by Sir Mix-A-Lot, 1989.)*

---

1. On the September 21, 1982 edition of "Good Morning America."
2. From her 1982 guidebook, "How to Deprogram Your Valley Girl."

wack *adjective* **LAME**, substandard, cracked, strange, inexplicable. Antonym of **FRESH**, **LEGIT**. Back-formation of "wacky" (crazy, offbeat, eccentric) which in turn likely derives from "out of whack" – malfunctioning, particularly of an ordered system normally reliant on balance or regularity that has now become disordered, unbalanced, or irregular. See also **WACKO**. *(Ref. "My Buddy" by DJ Jazzy Jeff & the Fresh Prince, 1988.)*

wack job *noun* A dangerously or unpleasantly crazy person. Derives from "wacky" (see **WACK**). See also **WACKO**. Also "whack job." *"It was no good. George Katz told you that. He said the guy was a wack job." (From "Trial Proceedings [...] in the case of the United States of America vs. Harrison A. Williams, Jr.,"* [1] *1981.)*

wacko *noun, adjective* As a noun, a crazy, eccentric person. Also "whacko." As an adjective, denoting such a nature. Of similar derivation to **WACK JOB**. However, "wacko" may be used as a backhanded compliment (signifying creative or entertaining eccentricity, as in the case of Michael Jackson's nickname "Wacko Jacko") whereas the term "wack job" is more likely to be found in a witness statement or insurance claim. *"I developed ["The Wacko Quotient" program] to test up to five wackos and average each of their scores." (From "Dr. C. Wacko Presents Applesoft BASIC and the Whiz-bang Miracle Machine" by David L. Heller, John F. Johnson, 1985.)*

wail *verb* Originally jazz slang to describe masterful, emotional playing of an instrument, particularly one that actually produces a wailing melody (i.e., human voice, saxophone, or trumpet; not drums). Later, the term's meaning expanded to include excellence or exuberant performance in any form and then, more figuratively, to greatness of any person or thing (e.g., "that jacket wails") in much the same manner of evolution as **ROCK** or **RULE**. *"Each little snail here know how to wail here." (From "The Little Mermaid," 1989.)*

waitron *noun* One who waits tables, the mechanical "-tron" suffix alluding to the robotic nature of the job. Sometimes humorously suggested as a gender-neutral alternative to "waiter"/"waitress." *"After a rough night in the Zone, you'll hit the nearest diner and ask your waitron for a large regular coffee." (From "On Language; Behind the Stick" by William Safire, "New York Times" magazine, May 3, 1981.)*

---

1. Another case related to the FBI's "Abscam" sting operation (see **MONEY TALKS AND BULLSHIT WALKS**, **SCAM**).

wang chung *verb* To enjoy oneself in a way that is not specifically defined but likely involves music and dancing. A phrase made briefly popular by its confounding inclusion in the song "Everybody Have Fun Tonight" by the eponymous **NEW WAVE** band. The phrase derives from ancient Chinese musicology and was included in the song both for self-referential commercial reasons and as a deliberately teasing nonsense term with mysterious Oriental overtones that could do duty for whatever positive meaning the listener wished to place on it. *(Ref. "Everybody Have Fun Tonight" by Wang Chung, 1986.)*

wannabe *noun* One who "wants to be" a member of a group or possessor of certain attributes, but who falls short due to a lack of talent, ability, courage, dedication, experience, etc. Primarily used within the spheres of artistic and criminal endeavor. See also **POSER**. *(Ref. "Mack Attack" by Too Short, 1989.)*

warm fuzzies *noun* Pleasant feelings initiated by positive stimulus from others such as physical touching, encouragement, praise, appreciation, applause, etc. *"He would continue working for warm fuzzies and warm fuzzies alone!" (From "The Independent Entertainer" by Happy Jack Feder, 1982.)*

warped *adjective* Degenerate or depraved. Often used as a compliment (see **SICK**). *"You used to be fun. You used to be warped and twisted and hilarious." (From "Say Anything…," 1989.)*

WASP *noun* An American of British descent, usually wealthy, often depicted as uptight and having an abnormal fondness for tweed. A White Anglo-Saxon Protestant. Often employed regardless of the subject's actual religion or specific ethnic origin, whiteness and money being the significant qualifications. See **PREPPY**.

wastoid *noun* A waster; one who fails to achieve anything close to his or her potential due to lack of effort and/or the attenuating effects of substance abuse. One for whom getting wasted results in a waste of time and opportunity. *"Yo, wastoid, you're not gonna blaze up in here!" (From "The Breakfast Club," 1985.)*

waver *noun* See **NEW-WAVER**.

way *interjection* Contradictory response to the expression of disbelief **NO WAY**: "On the contrary, that is in fact the case." Also "Yes way!" *"Oh, we got a problem." "No way!" "Yes, way." (From "The Monster Squad," 1987.)*

way cool *adjective* Extremely **COOL**.

wedgie *noun* See **MELVIN**.

weirdo *noun* One perceived by his peers to be odd. A favorite schoolyard insult. Differentiating the weirdo from the **NERD**, **GEEK**, or **DWEEB** is the fact that while the others' deficiencies are self-evident, clearly definable, and safely exploited, the weirdo is not so easily pinned down. This alienating mystique can occasionally lead to a degree of reluctant respect ("You never know, he might be oneathem **PSYCHO** types"). However, when employed by a female the term can be reliably interpreted to imply romantic rejection. *"Hey, it's the weirdo Weirdo, you got any cash for us today?" (From "The Neverending Story," 1984.)*

whacked *adjective* Under the influence of drugs and out of touch with the real world, like someone "whacked" (beaten) into an unconscious or delirious state. Also often "whacked out." One who is whacked may also be **WACK**: consequently the two terms, having a common ancestor but distinct derivation, were often used somewhat interchangeably. *"You're taking advantage. You know I'm whacked out on blood pressure medicine." (From "The Golden Girls" episode "Rose the Prude," 1985.)*

whammy bar *noun* The vibrato arm of an electric guitar or similar instrument, which modifies the pitch of the strings on the fly. The bar works by slackening the strings to deepen the note's pitch by moving the bridge forward (toward the neck) or tightening the strings to heighten the note's pitch by moving the bridge backward (away from the neck). *"It looks like your typical whammy bar. But this is MIDI. So it can control anything." (From "Keyboard" magazine, 1988.)*

whatchoo talkin' 'bout, Willis? *phrase* Catchphrase from the TV show "Diff'rent Strokes," uttered by the character Arnold (Gary Coleman) whenever baffled by his brother and consequently employed in similarly perplexing situations, with or without the terminal "Willis," by confused individuals.

whatever *interjection* **"whut-EVV-ur"** Dismissive, passive-aggressive, conversation-ending rejoinder. When used in the traditional positive sense the implication is that the speaker is open to all possibilities or happy with any choice previously presented; however, the negative sense defined here indicates that the speaker does not care about his or her interlocutor or anything that person has to say sufficiently to bother mustering enough energy to even disagree with him or her. Used as a universal retort by slow and/or lazy types, requiring no effort of wit. Seen by many as a tacit admission of having lost an argument. A favorite of teen **VALSPEAK** practitioners. *"The fact still is, I'm a dancer by nature." "Whatever." "Yeah, whatever." (From "Staying Alive," 1983.)*

what's your damage? *phrase* Inquiry requesting details of the mental or physical impairment that caused the subject to do whatever imbecilic, ignorant, malcoordinated, or inappropriate thing he or she just did. "What's your problem?" *[Heather bumps into Veronica] "What is your damage, Heather?" (From "Heathers," 1989.)*

where's the beef? *phrase* Slogan used to advertise Wendy's fast food restaurants, starting in 1984 and ending in '85, to position its burgers favorably in comparison to the big-name competitors: McDonald's Big Mac and Burger King's Whopper. Three old ladies examine an impressively large ("fluffy") hamburger bun but are disappointed to discover a minuscule beef patty within. The voice-over explains, "Some hamburger places give you a lot less beef on a lot of bun." The catchphrase was not only successful at selling burgers but entered the popular lexicon as a response to any situation in which one felt one was the victim of a bait-and-switch con or **SCAM** (being given something of less substance or lower quality than that advertised and paid for) or subject to flimflam obscuring the fact that something ostensibly significant was in fact insubstantial. The phrase was particularly popular in politics; in 1984 prospective presidential candidate (and former VP) Walter Mondale employed it to allege that his opponent Gary Hart's policies were ephemeral and feeble. *"Here you go, one cheeseburger platter." [...] "Uh-huh. I would like some meat in here." "Picky, picky. Hey, Pete. Where's the beef?" (From "The Muppets Take Manhattan," 1984.)*

whoa *interjection* Expression of surprise, sudden consternation, fear, or excitement. Originates from the traditional use of the word: a cry used to stop a horse and, by extension, to interrupt and pause a conversation (equivalent to "Wait a minute!"). The implication is that the speaker would like everything to stop happening for a while so he or she can fully appreciate whatever just happened. A favorite of the "Bill and Ted" characters. *"What did I do?" "You killed the car." "Whoa." (From "Ferris Bueller's Day Off," 1986.)*

wicked *adjective* Extremely good (amelioration; see **BAD**). Derives from the Old English "wicca" ("witch"). First used in its positive colloquial sense by F. Scott Fitzgerald in his 1920 debut novel "This Side of Paradise" to signify energetic or skillful dancing – "You two order; Phoebe and I are going to shake a wicked calf." In more general (teen, countercultural) usage in the 1960s and popular in the '80s. *"How was Joliet?" "Oh, it's bad. Thursday nights they serve a wicked pepper steak." (From "The Blues Brothers," 1980.)*

wigged *adjective* To have gone nuts (see **NUTBAR**) or to be out of touch with reality, particularly due to the effect of drugs. Also "wigged out." Derives from the older (1950s) slang "wig out," or "flip one's wig," which itself relies on the even older use of "wig" to refer to that which the hirsute prosthesis contains: the head, brain, and mind. *(Ref. "MTV – Get Off the Air" by Dead Kennedys, 1985.)*

wimp out *verb* To leave early or not show up at all, due to fear. In particular to disengage from a party or drinking session out of concern over intoxication. *"Prince Charming wimp out?" (From "Pretty in Pink," 1986.)*

wizard *noun* One possessing exceptional talent and skill or even complete mastery of a subject, profession, or endeavor. Particularly prevalent in the 1980s computing community, defined in the 1983 Jargon File (see **FLAME**) as one who "knows how a complex piece of software or hardware works." Also "wiz," "whiz." *(Ref. "Rock Box" by Run-DMC, 1984.)*

woody *noun* An erection. Also a vehicle with structural or ornamental elements constructed of timber, specifically the 1930s–50s station wagons popular with surfers since the 1950s, such as the 1940 Mercury Eight station wagon. Also "woodie." *"Oh, my goodness. I am sporting a tremendous woody right now." (From "Short Circuit," 1986.)*

word *interjection* Exclamation indicating sincere approval or assent. Often employed in emphasis of another's statement. Derives from the sense of "word" as vow, oath, or promise ("You have my word on that") popularized by the teachings of the Harlem-founded Five Percent Nation and, later, Zulu Nation: "Word is bond." Also used not only as an interrogative (i.e., "Is that really a fact?") but also as its reply (i.e., "Yes, that really is a fact") as follows: "[Statement]" "Word?" "Word." Originally **HIP HOP** slang, but more widespread in the late 1980s. *(Ref. "Ghetto Thang" by De La Soul, 1989.)*

word to your mother *phrase* **HIP HOP** expression, slight corruption of "Word to the mother," a gesture of respect referring to Africa, the motherland (as explained by Big Daddy Kane in his eponymous track: "I say the mother, as in the motherland"). Also, with "your," employed as a sly suggestion that the speaker is more familiar with one's mother than he has any right to be. While such an implication would certainly deserve a spot of educational wall-to-wall counseling it is frustratingly difficult to provably distinguish an insult from the serious and perfectly innocent usage of the phrase. *(Ref. "Ice Ice Baby" by Vanilla Ice, 1989.[1])*

word up *interjection* Injunction to listen up attentively or to speak out truthfully (**HIP HOP**). Also exclamation of assent; see **WORD**. *(Ref. "Word Up" by Cameo, 1986.)*

wuss *noun* A limp, malleable, spineless person; one who is both a wimp and a pussy. Also "wussy." *"You're being a wuss." "Wuss?" "Can it, Frank!" (From "The Monster Squad," 1987.)*

---

1. As B-side of "Play That Funky Music."

xlnt *adjective* **"zlint"** Excellent; an attempt to pronounce the classified advertisement abbreviation (e.g., "xlnt cond.") phonetically (note pronunciation). **VAL**-ish.

Y

yeah, that's the ticket *phrase* "Yeeeeaaah ... that's the ticket" Phrase popularized by Saturday Night Live character Tommy Flanagan (pronounced, flamboyantly, not "FLAN-ner-gan" but "Fla-NAY-gan"), self-proclaimed "President and Founder" of Pathological Liars Anonymous, played by John Lovitz. Flanagan would utter the line after spouting some highly improbable and entirely unconvincing lie, usually improved halfway through, such as "Yeah, I'm a producer, you know. Big-time telev– ... movie producer. Yeah, that's the ticket." Occasionally, as in the citation, the character remembers and attempts to hide his "tell." The phrase was thus used in everyday conversation to indicate that the speaker believed some blatant lie had just been spoken. Also "Yeah, that's it," "Yeaaaaah," and "Yeaaaaah, that's what happened." *"I'm here to tell ya that my client, Oliver North, is completely innocent, yeah. Ya know how I know? Cause ... uh ... cu ... it was me! Yeaaaaah, that's the ti ... uhh ... i-isn't that special?"[1] (From "Saturday Night Live," May 23, 1987.)*

yello *interjection* Portmanteau of "yes" (or "yeah") and "hello." Often used when answering the phone.

yes way *interjection* See WAY.

yikes *interjection* Exclamation of surprise and alarm. A derivation of the 18th century "yoicks!" (also "hoicks!") – a call to urge on the hounds during a hunt. *"Relax, I'll just throttle this baby back." [Throttle lever breaks off.] "Yikes!" (From "Howard the Duck," 1986.)*

yo *interjection* All-purpose greeting, exclamation demanding attention (equiv. "Hey!"), and affirmative. Used in English as a greeting since the mid-19th century, as a general cry since at least the 14th century. Also (with a short "o") Yiddish for "Yes" and (with emphasis on the first letter) Italian for "I." Common as an affirmative in the US military since WWII but brought into mainstream culture by way of Philadelphian Italian-American and African-American slang. Specifically, popularized by Sylvester Stallone in "Rocky," 1976: "Yo, Adrian! I did it!" *"How many Assholes we got on this ship, anyhow?" [All but a few crew-members stand up and reply loudly in unison.] "Yo!" (From "Spaceballs," 1987.)*

you know it *interjection* Affirmative; "You betcha!" Implies in an encouraging way that the answer is so definitely positive that the questioner should've known better than to even inquire. *"And you have*

---

1. See **ISN'T THAT SPECIAL?**

*a happy Thanksgiving." "Hey, you know it." (From "Planes, Trains & Automobiles,"
1987.)*

you're toast *phrase* See **TOAST**.

your mama *interjection* All-purpose but quite serious insult; abbreviation of "(Go) fuck your mama." A maternal insult, but distinct from
the "yo momma so fat" maternal insult jokes that became widely (sic)
popular in the early 1990s. *"Well, how do I look?" "Like shit, boss." [Pause.]
"Your mama." (From "Terminator," 1984.)*

yucky *adjective* Disgusting, nauseating. Infantile onomatopoeic term
preserved into adolescence by way of **VALSPEAK**. *"How's my boy, huh?
You having a good time at summer camp?" "Nah, it's yucky." (From "Cujo," 1983.)*

yuppie *noun* A "Young, Upwardly-mobile Professional" or "Young,
Urban Professional." A stereotypical presence in media throughout
the 1980s since the type's ascendancy in the early years of the
decade. Typically from a modest family background and now in his or
her twenties or thirties, the yuppie has achieved a level of material
and financial success by becoming a junior member of a well-paid
metropolitan profession (usually, post-college, as part of a corporate
structure; rarely as a solo entrepreneur). Essentially a simple soul, he
celebrates his ascent from studio apartments and ramen dinners by
indulging in and showing off his name-brand possessions. These
include cars (BMW 3 series – particularly the convertible; Porsche
928, 944, 911 on the upper end of the bell curve – particularly
cabriolet/targa; Benz 380SL; nothing domestic), clothing (Lauren,
Burberry, Armani, Lacoste, Brooks Brothers), accessories (Rolex,
Cartier, Coach, Gucci), and the visible accoutrements of approved
pastimes (squash rackets, stainless steel pasta machines, Krups
coffee makers, VCRs, Le Creuset cookware, Le Corbusier furniture,
Grolsch lager). While female examples exist in popular culture, the
male yuppie is often depicted preferring to consort with females
conforming more to **PREPPY** conventions. This is because the yuppie,
being by definition "upwardly mobile," seeks a mate occupying a
loftier social stratum than his own. The term "yuppie" became
popular after a 1982 article by Bob Greene described a **NETWORK**ing
event held by Jerry Rubin, formerly a leader of the radical Youth
International Party, whose followers were known as "yippies." The
story referred to attendees joking that Rubin had "gone from being a
yippie to being a yuppie." As with other socio-financial movements of
similar importance (see **PREPPY**), yuppiedom came with its own
popular explanatory manual: 1984's "The Yuppie Handbook: The
State-of-the-Art Manual for Young Urban Professionals." The
manual elegantly states that "the ultimate goal of a true yuppie is to
be his own role model." While there are certain stylistic crossovers
with prep, the difference between the yuppie and the preppy is more
fundamental than the obvious new/old money or urban/country
dichotomies: to imagine a yuppie, think of a preppy and remove
tradition, responsibility, and self-control. *"He's a yuppie, but he's so nice.
(From "Pretty in Pink," 1986.)*

yuppie flu *noun* Dismissive term for Chronic Fatigue Syndrome (also known as myalgic encephalomyelitis or ME). Often used to imply that the condition was attributable simply to professional "burnout" or, worse, "a fashionable form of hypochondria" ("Newsweek" magazine, November, 1990). *"I gained my first awareness of ME via the newspapers. It was being called 'the Yuppie disease' or 'Yuppie flu,' and was reported almost as a comic story." (From "ME and You" by Steve Wilkinson, 1988.)*

yuppify *verb* To screw up a place or activity by infesting it with YUPPIEs. In a less loaded sense, simply to gentrify or improve a place or thing or, of a person, to become a yuppie by means of improved education, financial stability, quality of life, etc. *"The consequence must be something more positive than exhortation to the broken and bewildered to yuppify themselves." (From "Election 87" by Eric Magee, 1988.)*

za and brew *phrase* Pizza and beer, the magical alliance that surpasses all other fine dining in inspiring optimism and defending the validity of the Leibnizian assertion that all is for the best in this best of all possible worlds. "Za," student slang dating from the late 1960s, is one of the rare occasions of a word being abbreviated from the head rather than the tail, likely adopted due to the pleasingly emphatic-sounding outcome and also the unsatisfactory results of trying to abbreviate "pizza" from the tail end. See also **BREW**.

zit *noun* A skin pustule, symptom of "acne vulgaris," indicative of poor bodily hygiene, immaturity (hormonal teenagerism), or both. *"I've got a cousin who went into dermatology. First year, sixty thousand." "Just for squeezing zits?" (From "Risky Business," 1983.)*

zlint *adjective* See **XLNT**.

zod *noun* A **WEIRDO**, an oddball in behavior or appearance, whose peculiarities are so pronounced as to be attributable only to extraterrestrial origin (see also **CONEHEAD**). The reference is likely to General Zod, antagonist of the movie "Superman II" (1980), played with uncanny menace by Terence Stamp. Another proposed derivation claims the term comes from "Izod," manufacturer of the famous alligator-logo polo shirts in the United States under license from Lacoste (until 1993). However, as these shirts were downright conventional and totally non-weird this theory is unlikely to be valid. *"This was spotted by Time magazine in a 1982 article by Michael Demarest on the language of California Valley Girls: 'People'd look at you and just go, 'Ew, she's a zod,' like get away.'" (From "On Language; The Derogator" by William Safire, "New York Times" magazine, July 28, 1985.)*

zone out *verb* To slip into a state of comfortable oblivion, commonly due to the anesthetic effects of television, long-winded oratory, etc.

The Yupper Hand

"He who dies with the most toys wins."

Who hasn't watched movies like "Wall Street" and "The Secret of My Success" (both 1987) and admired the wonderful life of the 1980s YUPPIE? Many fortunate readers may even have been among that elite class. Now you too can live or relive those golden years of voraciously acquisitive glory with this cut-out-and-play card game for two to six players!

Strive to collect as many classic '80s design icons as possible, which you can then boast about to other, less successful yuppies at dinner parties. Amassing everything from designer handbags and Swiss watches to state-of-the-art coffee makers and German luxury automobiles, only the most ruthless and skillful operator can gain "The Yupper Hand." Here's how to play:

1: Cut out (or photocopy and cut out) all thirty cards. If possible, laminate them or paste them onto cardstock backing for longevity. Make them all look as similar as possible so cardshark players can't tell who has which cards.

2: One player is the dealer. The dealer shuffles the cards and deals an equal number of cards to each player (including him/herself), face down. If there are cards left over, set them aside without revealing them.

3: The players pick up their stacks of cards, not letting the other players see. Play commences to the left of the dealer and proceeds clockwise.

4: Each possession has been scientifically assigned statistical scores for six categories of enviable desirability: Cost, Exclusivity, Shininess, Design Factor, Utility, and Coolness. The player to the dealer's left looks at his or her top card and chooses one of the categories on which to compete (higher scores are better). He or she then states the possession's name and brashly challenges the other players with the relevant boast. For example, "Mercedes-Benz five-sixty SEL.... Exclusivity – Nine!"

5: The other players in turn read out their top card's score for the chosen category.

6: The player with the highest score in the chosen category wins, taking the losing cards from the other players and placing them at the bottom of his or her stack of cards.

7: Play continues, with the next player choosing the category on which the next cards compete, and so on.

8: A player who runs out of cards is "out" and is officially a loser. The player who successfully acquires all the possessions is the winner!

POSSESSION:
BMW 320i Cabriolet

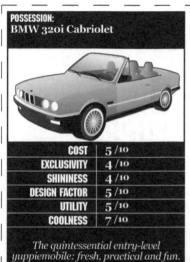

COST	5 /10
EXCLUSIVITY	4 /10
SHININESS	4 /10
DESIGN FACTOR	5 /10
UTILITY	5 /10
COOLNESS	7 /10

The quintessential entry-level yuppiemobile: fresh, practical and fun.

POSSESSION:
Sony Walkman

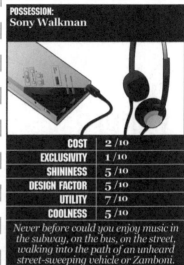

COST	2 /10
EXCLUSIVITY	1 /10
SHININESS	5 /10
DESIGN FACTOR	5 /10
UTILITY	7 /10
COOLNESS	5 /10

Never before could you enjoy music in the subway, on the bus, on the street, walking into the path of an unheard street-sweeping vehicle or Zamboni.

POSSESSION:
Giorgio Armani Two-Piece Suit

COST	3 /10
EXCLUSIVITY	4 /10
SHININESS	6 /10
DESIGN FACTOR	8 /10
UTILITY	5 /10
COOLNESS	8 /10

Lightweight, loose, sharp but casual, a rakish hint of the louche: the suit's characteristics reflect on its wearer.

POSSESSION:
Rolex Datejust Steel & Gold

COST	4 /10
EXCLUSIVITY	7 /10
SHININESS	9 /10
DESIGN FACTOR	4 /10
UTILITY	6 /10
COOLNESS	5 /10

Rolex says you value quality and tradition. Datejust says you're a focused professional. Steel and gold says it's the 1980s.

CUT OUT & PLAY

THE
YUPPER
HAND®

He who dies with the most toys wins.*

THE
YUPPER
HAND®

He who dies with the most toys wins.*

THE
YUPPER
HAND®

He who dies with the most toys wins.*

THE
YUPPER
HAND®

He who dies with the most toys wins.*

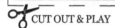 CUT OUT & PLAY

POSSESSION:
Effervescent Mineral Water

COST	1 /10
EXCLUSIVITY	1 /10
SHININESS	5 /10
DESIGN FACTOR	5 /10
UTILITY	7 /10
COOLNESS	6 /10

Imported, carbonated, flinty, sophisticated. Better for you than the lunchtime martini.

POSSESSION:
Ralph Lauren Ladies' Power Suit

COST	3 /10
EXCLUSIVITY	4 /10
SHININESS	4 /10
DESIGN FACTOR	8 /10
UTILITY	7 /10
COOLNESS	6 /10

Big shoulders, wasp waist and pencil skirt mean business.

POSSESSION:
Converted Warehouse Loft Apartment

COST	9 /10
EXCLUSIVITY	5 /10
SHININESS	2 /10
DESIGN FACTOR	6 /10
UTILITY	4 /10
COOLNESS	9 /10

Floor-to-ceiling windows, exposed brickwork, pipes and wiring, erratic vintage freight elevators: edgy urban living at its finest, with a cost to match.

POSSESSION:
Porsche 928

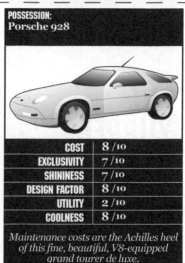

COST	8 /10
EXCLUSIVITY	7 /10
SHININESS	7 /10
DESIGN FACTOR	8 /10
UTILITY	2 /10
COOLNESS	8 /10

Maintenance costs are the Achilles heel of this fine, beautiful, V8-equipped grand tourer de luxe.

✂ CUT OUT & PLAY

THE YUPPER HAND

He who dies with the most toys wins.

THE YUPPER HAND

He who dies with the most toys wins.

THE YUPPER HAND

He who dies with the most toys wins.

THE YUPPER HAND

He who dies with the most toys wins.

 CUT OUT & PLAY

POSSESSION:
Giant, Hideous Abstract Painting

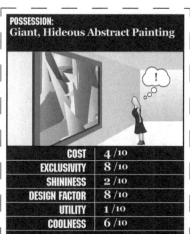

COST	4 /10
EXCLUSIVITY	8 /10
SHININESS	2 /10
DESIGN FACTOR	8 /10
UTILITY	1 /10
COOLNESS	6 /10

Anyone who says they don't like it clearly just doesn't understand art, dahling. The philistines.

POSSESSION:
Wharton M.B.A.

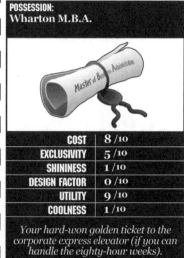

COST	8 /10
EXCLUSIVITY	5 /10
SHININESS	1 /10
DESIGN FACTOR	0 /10
UTILITY	9 /10
COOLNESS	1 /10

Your hard-won golden ticket to the corporate express elevator (if you can handle the eighty-hour weeks).

POSSESSION:
Volvo 740 Wagon

COST	5 /10
EXCLUSIVITY	5 /10
SHININESS	1 /10
DESIGN FACTOR	6 /10
UTILITY	9 /10
COOLNESS	No

Famous for its safety, this boxy Swedish auto is the #1 choice of the conscientious, successful yuppie parent. So practical it's also a preppy favorite.

POSSESSION:
Krups Coffina Coffee Grinder

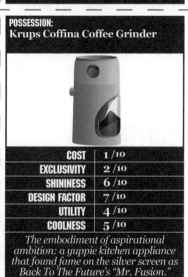

COST	1 /10
EXCLUSIVITY	2 /10
SHININESS	6 /10
DESIGN FACTOR	7 /10
UTILITY	4 /10
COOLNESS	5 /10

The embodiment of aspirational ambition: a yuppie kitchen appliance that found fame on the silver screen as Back To The Future's "Mr. Fusion."

✂ CUT OUT & PLAY

THE YUPPER HAND®

He who dies with the most toys wins.*

THE YUPPER HAND®

He who dies with the most toys wins.*

THE YUPPER HAND®

He who dies with the most toys wins.*

THE YUPPER HAND®

He who dies with the most toys wins.*

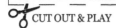 CUT OUT & PLAY

POSSESSION:
Mercedes-Benz 380SL Convertible

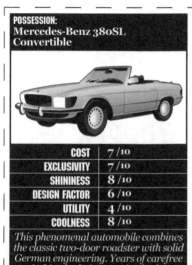

COST	7 /10
EXCLUSIVITY	7 /10
SHININESS	8 /10
DESIGN FACTOR	6 /10
UTILITY	4 /10
COOLNESS	8 /10

This phenomenal automobile combines the classic two-door roadster with solid German engineering. Years of carefree wind-in-the-hair motoring beckon.

POSSESSION:
Swatch Watch

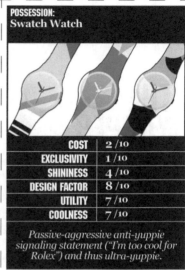

COST	2 /10
EXCLUSIVITY	1 /10
SHININESS	4 /10
DESIGN FACTOR	8 /10
UTILITY	7 /10
COOLNESS	7 /10

Passive-aggressive anti-yuppie signaling statement ("I'm too cool for Rolex") and thus ultra-yuppie.

POSSESSION:
Gucci Horsebit Loafers

COST	4 /10
EXCLUSIVITY	4 /10
SHININESS	8 /10
DESIGN FACTOR	7 /10
UTILITY	2 /10
COOLNESS	4 /10

Beautifully-made Italian footwear fit for only the cleanest city sidewalk in the finest weather and entirely impractical for anything else.

POSSESSION:
Incomprehensible Metal Sculpture

COST	5 /10
EXCLUSIVITY	9 /10
SHININESS	8 /10
DESIGN FACTOR	7 /10
UTILITY	2 /10
COOLNESS	7 /10

Massive enough to inspire concerns about the building's structural integrity. Not entirely impractical; your guests can hang their coats on it.

CUT OUT & PLAY

**THE
YUPPER
HAND**™

He who dies with the most toys wins.™

**THE
YUPPER
HAND**™

He who dies with the most toys wins.™

**THE
YUPPER
HAND**™

He who dies with the most toys wins.™

**THE
YUPPER
HAND**™

He who dies with the most toys wins.™

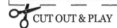 CUT OUT & PLAY

THE
YUPPER
HAND®

He who dies with the most toys wins.®

THE
YUPPER
HAND®

He who dies with the most toys wins.®

THE
YUPPER
HAND®

He who dies with the most toys wins.®

THE
YUPPER
HAND®

He who dies with the most toys wins.®

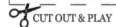 CUT OUT & PLAY

THE DICTIONARY OF 1980S SLANG

POSSESSION:
Cartier Ladies' Tank Watch

COST	4 /10
EXCLUSIVITY	6 /10
SHININESS	8 /10
DESIGN FACTOR	6 /10
UTILITY	6 /10
COOLNESS	7 /10

Perhaps the most elegant, iconic and historic wristwatch ever made, this timepiece was originally designed for a man but looks better on a woman.

POSSESSION:
Porsche 944

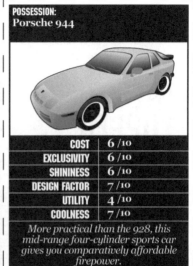

COST	6 /10
EXCLUSIVITY	6 /10
SHININESS	6 /10
DESIGN FACTOR	7 /10
UTILITY	4 /10
COOLNESS	7 /10

More practical than the 928, this mid-range four-cylinder sports car gives you comparatively affordable firepower.

POSSESSION:
Psychoanalysis

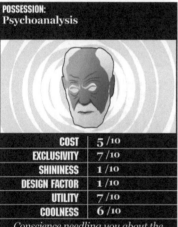

COST	5 /10
EXCLUSIVITY	7 /10
SHININESS	1 /10
DESIGN FACTOR	1 /10
UTILITY	7 /10
COOLNESS	6 /10

Conscience needling you about the corporate villainy and ruthless social triage required to acquire a key to the executive washroom? Not any more.

POSSESSION:
Bespoke Three-Piece Business Suit

COST	4 /10
EXCLUSIVITY	6 /10
SHININESS	3 /10
DESIGN FACTOR	7 /10
UTILITY	6 /10
COOLNESS	6 /10

A tailored navy pin-stripe three-piece informs the observer that you are a personage of serious substance, not to be trifled with.

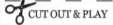
CUT OUT & PLAY

THE YUPPER HAND™

He who dies with the most toys wins.*

THE YUPPER HAND™

He who dies with the most toys wins.*

THE YUPPER HAND™

He who dies with the most toys wins.*

THE YUPPER HAND™

He who dies with the most toys wins.*

✂ CUT OUT & PLAY

POSSESSION:
Manhattan Condo

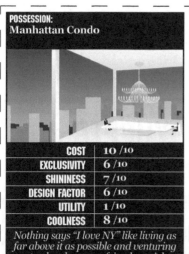

COST	10 /10
EXCLUSIVITY	6 /10
SHININESS	7 /10
DESIGN FACTOR	6 /10
UTILITY	1 /10
COOLNESS	8 /10

Nothing says "I love NY" like living as far above it as possible and venturing out only when your friends can't be persuaded to bring you groceries.

POSSESSION:
Gold Rolex Day-Date

COST	6 /10
EXCLUSIVITY	10 /10
SHININESS	10 /10
DESIGN FACTOR	5 /10
UTILITY	5 /10
COOLNESS	1 /10

Justifiably nicknamed "The President." For "the man whose life is an event," ran the advertisements.

POSSESSION:
Mercedes-Benz 560SEL

COST	8 /10
EXCLUSIVITY	9 /10
SHININESS	8 /10
DESIGN FACTOR	4 /10
UTILITY	3 /10
COOLNESS	6 /10

A long-wheelbase S-Class tells the world you've truly arrived. The favorite of puppet dictators and third-world royalty the world over.

POSSESSION:
Coach Handbag

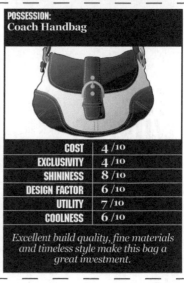

COST	4 /10
EXCLUSIVITY	4 /10
SHININESS	8 /10
DESIGN FACTOR	6 /10
UTILITY	7 /10
COOLNESS	6 /10

Excellent build quality, fine materials and timeless style make this bag a great investment.

✂ CUT OUT & PLAY

THE YUPPER HAND

He who dies with the most toys wins.*

THE YUPPER HAND

He who dies with the most toys wins.*

THE YUPPER HAND

He who dies with the most toys wins.*

THE YUPPER HAND

He who dies with the most toys wins.*

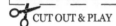 CUT OUT & PLAY

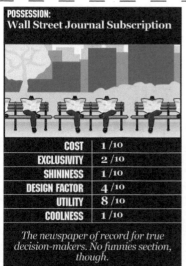

POSSESSION:
Wall Street Journal Subscription

COST	1 /10
EXCLUSIVITY	2 /10
SHININESS	1 /10
DESIGN FACTOR	4 /10
UTILITY	8 /10
COOLNESS	1 /10

The newspaper of record for true decision-makers. No funnies section, though.

POSSESSION:
Live-In Housekeeper

COST	5 /10
EXCLUSIVITY	7 /10
SHININESS	2 /10
DESIGN FACTOR	1 /10
UTILITY	8 /10
COOLNESS	2 /10

The ultimate redundant luxury: a domestic servant in a home full of labor-saving gadgets.

 CUT OUT & PLAY

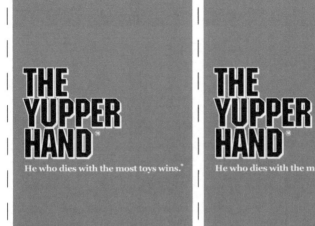

 CUT OUT & PLAY

Made in United States
Troutdale, OR
08/19/2023

12199918R10086